Y0-BZD-820

TEENS
A Fresh Look

MOTHERING MAGAZINE

*Edited by Anne Pedersen
and Peggy O'Mara*

John Muir Publications
Santa Fe, New Mexico

John Muir Publications, P.O. Box 613, Santa Fe, NM 87504

© 1991 by Mothering Magazine
Cover © 1991 by John Muir Publications
All rights reserved. Published 1991
Printed in the United States of America

First edition. First printing

Library of Congress Cataloging-in-Publication Data

Teens : a fresh look / Mothering magazine : edited by Anne Pedersen
and Peggy O'Mara. — 1st ed.
    p. cm.
Includes bibliographical references and index.
ISBN 0-945465-54-8
1. Parent and teenager—United States. I. Pedersen, Anne, 1949
II. O'Mara, Peggy. III. Mothering.
HQ799.15.T44 1991   90-25425
305.23'5—dc20   CIP

Mothering Magazine, P.O. Box 1690, Santa Fe, NM 87504
    Subscriptions: P.O. Box 532, Mt. Morris, IL 61054

Chapter 1, "Adolescence Is Not a Terminal Disease," © 1990 by Eda LeShan.
    Originally appeared in *Mothering*.
Chapter 3, "Character Development during Adolescence," adapted with permission
    from Betty K. Staley, *Between Form and Freedom: A Practical Guide to the Teenage
    Years* (Stroud, U.K.: Hawthorn, 1988).
Chapter 5, "The Changes of Puberty: Talking to Teens about What's Happening to
    Their Bodies," adapted from The *"What's Happening to My Body?" Book for Girls*
    and The *"What's Happening to My Body?" Book for Boys*, by Lynda Madaras.
    © 1983, 1988 and 1984, 1988, respectively, by Lynda Madaras. Reprinted by
    permission of Newmarket Press, 18 East 48 Street, New York, NY 10017.

Distributed to the book trade by
W. W. Norton & Company, Inc.
New York, New York

Design: Sally Blakemore
Typographer: Copygraphics, Inc.
Printer: McNaughton & Gunn, Inc.

Cover based on photo by Lisa Law

CONTENTS

FOREWORD

There is a need for this book. I see it in the anxious eyes of the father who raises his hand during my parent workshop and asks, "What do you do about teenagers?" I hear it in the jokes and nervous laughter that follow the question. ("Lock 'em in a closet and don't let 'em out until they turn twenty!") I hear it in the warnings given young mothers by parents of grown children: "Enjoy them now while they're still small," or "Little children, little problems; big children, big problems." I see it in newspaper reports about the rise in teen pregnancy, substance abuse, depression, and suicide; in the well-publicized decline in student achievement; and in family sit-coms in which parents discuss the antics of their rebellious adolescents as they roll their eyes heavenward. From every source the message is the same and the message is clear: these sweet, adorable children, "Jeckylls" all, will one day turn into monstrous "Hydes," with insatiable appetites, wild mood swings, and inexplicable, often revolting, behavior.

The recollection of our own adolescence usually does little to dispel our fears. Who among us dwells lovingly upon the memory of the excruciating anxieties of his or her teenage years? Most of us are happy to be done with those painful times and are not at all eager to relive our adolescent angst through our own children.

Along comes *Teens: A Fresh Look* to the rescue. It is just what its title promises and more—a vision of adolescence as a time of growth and opportunity for both parents and children. This collection of voices—some well-known, like David Elkind and Eda LeShan, others perhaps less familiar—informs, reassures, entertains, and inspires us. Lynda Madaras writes with delightful style and candor about how to help young people come to terms with their changing bodies. A poignant account by Lorraine Vissering takes us inside the head and heart of a fifteen-year-old who is having her first baby. Don Dinkmeyer reviews the basics of what makes for caring communication with teenagers, and Mitch Bobrow tackles the same subject from a more personal point of view. From Susannah Sheffer we learn how we can help our youngsters formulate their career goals. Robert Schwebel makes clear the limitations of the "just say no" approach to drugs and alcohol and suggests sensible alternatives. Elizabeth Hormann convinces us that even "good families can have troubled children" and outlines a plan of action that offers hope to the whole family. Punctuating the broad range of essays—some warm and funny, some sober and scholarly—are poems that slice through to essential truths so swiftly that we smile in instant recognition.

By the time you come to the end of this volume, I suspect that much of the fear of coping with the adolescents in your life will have dissipated. The challenge of how to relate to this strange creature called a "teenager" and help him or her metamorphose into an adult will have been clarified and reduced to a manageable size and shape. Armed with new information, insight, and attitudes, you'll be ready to say, "Bring on your worst case of adolescence. I'm prepared."

—*Adele Faber*

INTRODUCTION

Coming of Age in America

Peggy O'Mara

Today I watched my teenage son and two of his friends run barefoot out to the hammock. It's early fall and cold, and the way to
the hammock is rocky, but I could tell that it was important to them
to do it, to know that they could walk on the rocks barefoot. The boys
have been camping out on our land the last two nights. The first
night, they braved three hours in the tent while the worst thunder
and lightning storm of the season crashed outside. Later, when they
finally came into the house soaked, they admitted that the water had
been running under the tent and dripping in their faces, but as they
jokingly said, they endured it because they were "being men."

These boys are living out a rite of passage. While many may complain that our modern lives are devoid of meaningful rituals, I am confident that young people will invent those rituals they need to come of
age in the United States today.

The popular press tends to portray teens in a very deprecating way.
A recent *Newsweek* special edition on adolescence gave the impression that most teens are experimenting with drugs, alcohol, and sex
and are overly concerned with fashion and vulgar music. Sound
familiar? Of course it does. But just who are these teens? Am I naive
because I live in a small town, or is this stereotype just another generation's way of trivializing and condescending to the teen experience?
The truth is that teens *are* too much for most people to handle, not
because they are into drugs, sex, and fashion but because they reflect
so clearly the inconsistencies and ambiguities of adult life.

Adults and teens are involved in an intimate transfer of power.
Alternately, teens grab for power, then refuse it. Alternately, we are
eager to give it up and jealous of its loss. This is the stuff of the adolescent years. It cannot be avoided by better parenting. In fact, to avoid

it may be to ensure difficulty with power and authority later in life.

Why a book about teens? Because we *need* a fresh look at teens. At a time when children need clear direction and moral leadership from us, we often dismiss their behavior as merely a product of overactive hormones, or we avoid asserting our own authority with them for fear of confrontation. And we are arrogant. As a generation of parents who have tried to be conscious mothers and fathers and who remember the pain of our own childhoods, we have allowed ourselves to believe that if we parented "right," our children would be spared the turmoil of the teen years. And we have judged other families who have had trouble with their teens harshly, believing we could avoid such problems through virtuous parenting. What we often fail to understand is that the power struggle between teens and adults is necessary for the child to become an adult. It goes with the territory.

The parent-child relationship during adolescence resembles the weaning process of the bear cub. The mother bear is a devoted mother and teaches her cubs to obey her unconditionally. One day, she takes her cubs to a tree and, in effect, tells them to climb up it and not to come down under any circumstances. Then the mother bear leaves and never comes back. In order to survive, the bear cubs have to disobey their mother.

In the United States today, we are confused about disobedience. On the one hand, we disapprove of the often harmless rebellion manifested by teen clothes, hairstyles, and music. On the other hand, we are ineffectual in responding to the more dangerous temptations of drugs, alcohol, sex, and suicide. We need a new look at teens because we need to better understand the adolescent experience. Then we can stop taking their behavior personally and can respond to our teenagers as the elders they expect us to be.

Teens are like two-year-olds. They have excellent boundaries. Remember the dance teacher who tells the preschool dance class to imagine a balloon around each of them that separates each dancer from the others? Teens know about this balloon. They know what is their business and what is yours. They have a healthy narcissism; they know their preferences and sometimes cannot be reasoned with regarding them. And they are highly self-conscious. Often it's as if they've just awakened from a dream and realized that they were here. This is why many teens go through a black phase in the early teen years. For a while, they dye their hair black and wear black lipstick

Photo by John Schoenwalter Photography

and nail polish, black T-shirts, and long, black coats. They are in hiding.

Teens also have a healthy rebelliousness. For the first time, they see the life of their own family with some degree of objectivity. They then have to reconcile this new knowledge with their love for their family and their growing attachment to their peers. They are not quite sure who they are, but they are absolutely sure of who they are not. They are creating themselves.

This teen rebelliousness is often difficult for parents to deal with because it challenges them at a time when they may be in a state of flux themselves. Adolescence runs parallel to "middle-essence," a time when parents may be reevaluating their own lives. The teens are thrusting outward; the parents are looking inward. The teens want to embellish; the parents to simplify. This counterpoint is probably necessary. It keeps the parents from getting too introspective and serious and helps the teens keep their feet on the ground.

The other day, I spoke to a father who thought his four-year-old was a brat because it took her forever to put away her toys and she talked back to him. "But she's supposed to be a brat," I thought. Teens are brats, too. And they're supposed to be. They are stubborn, intractable, rude, unaware of others' needs, difficult to talk to, and emotionally volatile. In short, they have excellent boundaries. It is precisely these emerging boundaries, so well defined, that we adults find infuriating. We are used to and much prefer acquiescence from our children. We believe that giving in to other people is kinder than resistance, and we hope we have raised our children to be kind. The wise parent will encourage this healthy boundary development. At the same time, he or she will provide structure and set limits that reflect what real life is like and provide balance to the unlimited possibilities the teen feels inside.

It is in understanding and having compassion for the teen experience that we parents and adults can best respond to it. The teen years are necessarily a time of upheaval. This upheaval is part of the transformation from child to adult and from dependent to independent. The teen is neither child nor adult; the teen is in "nor" time. In "nor" time, all is experienced with a sense of heightened awareness. The protective veil of the family parts a bit, and the teen sees that there is a discrepancy between what people say and what they do. This necessary loss of innocence begins the process of unfolding awareness so vital to the emerging adult. And consciousness is never won without suffering. Despite likely changes of mood and lack of response from their teen, wise parents continue to act as a bumper rail on the bridge to maturity that their child is driving across.

Parenting is mostly strategy. You hope for some modicum of control but also know that anything can happen. When our children are babies, there is only so far they can go, and our world with them appears protected. When they are teens, our world with them is infinite. We know that our teens are vulnerable; they feel invincible. We think of teens as *having arrived* somewhere, when in fact, it has just occurred to them that they are *going* somewhere. Having discovered this, they want to get to that "somewhere" as soon as possible. We can no longer protect them all of the time and begin to realize that we will have to learn to live without them sooner than we thought.

Being a parent of a teen requires great reserves of confidence, self-esteem, and resiliency—if for no other reason than to be able to confront six tall young men in a messy kitchen and demand that they clean it up. Being a parent of a teen requires a willingness to claim your authority as a parent and to insist on the right and responsibility to protect your teens even when they don't want protection. And being a parent of a teen requires developing a sense of humor. Life with teens can be very funny. As Dorothy Parker said, "The best way to keep children home is make the home atmosphere pleasant—and let the air out of the tires."

PART I:
TEENS AND THE WORLD

Photo by Marilyn Nolt

1

ADOLESCENCE IS NOT

A TERMINAL DISEASE

Eda LeShan

I have recently been spending some time answering letters from teenagers about all the terrible and tragic events of their lives. Things like pimples, or being too tall or too short, or being in love with the boy who loves someone else, or being too shy to ask the girl you like to the school dance—you know, all the earthshaking agonies of being young.

After a couple of days of reading these sorrowful, even hysterical cries for help, I began to feel a little shaken myself and decided I'd better stop and take a rest. I began having the sneaky feeling that maybe these kids are right; maybe being thirteen or fourteen or fifteen really is the end of the world.

Two facts helped me to recover a sense of perspective: remembering being an adolescent myself and remembering being the mother of one! I still have a little black diary (with lock and key) into which I poured my thoughts and feelings at the age of fifteen. There were ecstatic highs (Frederick March *smiled* at me when he gave me his autograph!) and suicidal lows (when I got 6% on a math test and the boy I loved madly ignored me completely at a school dance). I wanted to kill my mother when she told me I couldn't go to a movie until I'd cleaned up my room, and I wanted to kill myself when I lied to her and she was understanding and compassionate. After a terrible crisis during which I yelled at both my parents that I absolutely positively would rather die than go to a family party—and they accepted my decision and went off without me—I wrote, "Why am I such a terrible person? I am going to crawl into bed and cry my heart out. I don't think I will ever get over being such a mean, cruel, awful person. If nobody ever loves me, I will understand it."

By the time I was the mother of a teenager, I had managed to repress

Photo by Michael Weisbrot

memories of my own adolescent, end-of-the-world attitudes. But by the time my daughter was thirteen, I was feeling the same way again—with a new twist. The world would never be endurable again because my child hated me so much; because she was the slob of all time; because she lied; because she wouldn't be seen dead at a family gathering. What had my husband and I done wrong to create such an unhappy, rebellious, miserable child? It was, once again, time to crawl into bed and cry.

It is comforting to realize that both my daughter and I are now decent, responsible, loving and loved adults. Our adolescent years did neither of us in. But there is no question that adolescence is pretty hard on everyone. The process by which a child's body and mind move over the bridge into adulthood is the most chaotic and dramatic growth process imaginable outside of that which starts the moment an eager sperm meets a friendly egg.

The hormonal upheaval alone is enough to turn the nicest kid into a raving maniac. If you add to those physiological facts all the turmoil of trying to figure out how to be a reasonably mature adult in this insane and terrifying world, it is not too hard to figure out why our children get fixated on pimples. It's certainly partly because the real issues of growth from childhood to adulthood are almost too much for anyone to handle, least of all someone who has only had twelve or thirteen years of experience in living.

Helping one's child live through these turbulent years—and helping oneself to survive—calls for a balancing act worthy of Barnum & Bailey's best acrobats. What is called for is sympathy and compassion—without hysteria. What sometimes happens is that parents themselves become so distraught that they confirm the child's own sense of disaster. What is needed is something on the order of, "I know how you are suffering, my poor darling—I remember feeling the same way myself—*but nobody ever died of adolescence.*"

Nobody ever dies from merely *being* thirteen or fourteen or fifteen. But some teenagers do die from drugs and suicide. Things have changed since I was a teenager in the 1930s; they've even changed since my daughter was a teenager in the 1960s. There are new terrors to deal with: the threat of nuclear war and environmental poisons, extreme academic pressure and competitiveness, and an increased prevalence of alcohol and drugs. Now, parents have to be more than compassionate and understanding. They must be attentive, observant, and able to express their love and concern consistently and honestly.

One of the most important lessons to be learned during the early years of puberty is that any kind of growth that's worth having causes struggle and pain. The only way in which we move on to deeper levels of self-understanding, personal fulfillment, and more creative relationships and work is through periods of great vulnerability, of feeling all shook up. This process of change is not dangerous or destructive. Quite the reverse: it is the birth of a new self. Self-consciousness, shyness, tremendous mood swings, feelings of fury and sadness, frustration and terror, ecstasy—or just having the giggles—are part of growing up. To give up the safety and comfort of being cared for by grown-ups in order to begin to take responsibility for one's own life takes tremendous courage. It is a sign of remarkable fortitude that any child fights so hard for the questionable privilege of being an independent adult in a confusing and often frightening world.

The best help a parent can give an adolescent is availability. We need to let our children know we are here to help pick up the pieces when things go wrong—when they're not invited to the prom, when they choose a boyfriend or girlfriend who creates trouble for them, when they try out for a team sport that's not suited to their particular skills. But parents shouldn't stand in the way of the experimentation that's a necessary part of learning for oneself. I think most of us would concede we learned far more from our mistakes than we did from our successes. Young people desperately need the right to make their own mistakes—even some beauts, if necessary—so long as these mistakes are not dangerous to health and safety.

When all is said and done, what every teenager needs is parents who can roll with the punches—mothers and fathers who do not take slurs personally, who avoid getting sucked into wild moods of elation and depression, and who are always available for crises without saying, "I told you so."

2

THE EMERGING

ADOLESCENT

Joyce Roby Belanger

More than fourteen years of teaching eleven- and twelve-year-olds has taught me a great deal about the transitional years between childhood and adolescence. Much has been written about the changes children go through during their teenage years, and parents of adolescents often steel themselves for tumult during this time. However, when the preteen child begins to go through unexpected changes, parents can be unprepared. As varied as children are, there are some changes unique to this time of life that virtually all kids go through.

Signs of Change

Parents who suspect that a particular "problem" is surfacing in their home should be relieved to learn that much the same situation exists in other preteen homes.

Appearance. One striking change that begins to occur at this age is that children become much more concerned about the way they look. Gone is the boy who used to let the shower run while he sat fully dressed on the stool. He now spends time preening in front of the mirror or locked in the bathroom, practicing his smile. This new desire for cleanliness and a pleasing appearance seems to coincide with a budding awareness of the opposite sex.

Whatever particular style the eleven-year-old chooses to adopt for his or her look, it is sacred territory and not to be interfered with by unthinking adults. Charles had a wonderful head of hair that I always managed to pat as I passed. One day he seemed particularly grumpy, and when I smoothed his head, he barked that he hated it when I touched his hair because it messed it up. That day I learned an important lesson in respect. Most preteen children have a special way they

Photo by Marilyn Nolt

want their hair to look and may go through elaborate rituals of blow-drying, moussing, combing, and spraying to arrange it just so. Why disturb such a masterpiece?

Imaginary Audience. Preteens often react to what one of my colleagues terms an "imaginary audience." This audience watches every move they make. A student may worry that she stayed in the rest room too long and that the audience probably noticed the lapse of time. She may also imagine that the audience watched her leave, noticed that her hem was flipped up, and observed how she straightened her blouse. Boys take to wearing their shirttails out to help cover uncivilized erections, while girls check into the rest room frequently to make sure that their periods have not yet come.

The imaginary audience not only observes preteens; it laughs at them, hears them out, and aids them in acting out mental fantasies. I sometimes wonder how they can concentrate at all on their academics with such a rich and active inner life!

Growth. Eleven- and twelve-year-olds often grow in odd ways. Arms and legs can develop at varying rates of speed, making for gangly bodies. Even though the resulting clumsy appearance may last for only a month or so, this can be an intense time. Whatever area seems to be growing disproportionately—often the hands or feet—the emerging teenager is concerned about it. One student I taught a few years back endured several months of silent turmoil before telling anyone that he thought he was turning into a woman. It seems that his breasts were puffing slightly. A trip to the doctor confirmed that this development is completely normal for boys his age.

Girls who are taller than their classmates may fear that they will never stop growing. Short boys are equally miserable. The first girl who needs a bra vascillates between a new sense of pride and the uncomfortable realization that no one else has one. And late bloomers may carry their uncertainties for several years to come.

Concern. "Overly concerned" is an understatement for what seems to roll around in the minds of preteens. James calmly asked his parents to tell him, truthfully, if he had any incurable diseases that they had not yet informed him of. He was now prepared to hear the truth. Thank goodness his parents did not burst out laughing; instead, they realized the burden he had been carrying around and discussed the matter with him.

I remember thinking, at around age twelve, that I must have been adopted because there were very few baby pictures of me. I was certain that my parents had been lying to me all along. To make matters worse, my older sisters, in hysterics, egged me on.

What's more, children of this age group tend to be concerned not only about their own looks, personalities, and fears but also about *your* looks, personality, and fears! For example, they begin to tell their parents how to dress, not to kiss them in front of their friends, or to be silent while car pooling.

Organization and Sequence. Although emerging adolescents are beginning to recognize a world outside of the self, they are not yet fully reasonable in their evaluations of it. Possibilities of catastrophe loom larger than life, and unfortunate circumstances seem imminent. Life experience has not yet taken on an organized sequence. It is now that children begin to really understand the inevitability of death, and many worry greatly about the death of family members, even if there is no apparent provocation. When someone they know is sick, they may imagine the illness to be much worse than it is. Just as our generation of preteens was convinced that girls could become pregnant by drinking from a water fountain, so today's preteens are convinced of their vulnerability to AIDS and other epidemics—a phenomenon surely enhanced by their exposure to widespread misinformation.

Sharing the probability, organization, and sequence of actions with our children will serve to guide them through the coming years and help them to put events in perspective. When there are news reports of a burglar in a certain neighborhood, for instance, preteens have been known to spend the night awake, listening to every noise and convinced that the thief is at their house. In such a situation, explaining the odds and talking about safety precautions will provide your nighttime listener with a helpful inner dialogue, if not belief.

Fear of the Unknown. Fear of the unknown, coupled with worrisome absorptions, causes preteens many sleepless nights. Sixth grade seems to be a time of life when students frequently report an inability to sleep at night. (And one look at them shows it!) About one-third of my class generally does not sleep. So, be prepared for a wakeful year, as twelve-year-olds spend many silent night hours wondering, worrying, and thinking.

Emotions. The dramatics of the eleven- or twelve-year-old can be entertaining in hindsight but exasperating in the present. Their dis-

Photo by Michael Weisbrot

plays of emotion are outstanding performances! This is not to say that the emotion is feigned, just that it tends to be overdramatized.

An inconsolably weeping Marta confided to her mother one night that all the children had laughed at something she had said in school. When her concerned mother and I talked, I related that two of the more popular girls had laughed. To a sensitive preteen, however, "everybody" consists of anyone of importance. This sense of drama often evokes the time-worn saying, "But *everyone* else gets to go! Even Steven gets to go, and his mom is way more strict than you!" When sorting through the "everybodys," a parent will usually find that they are really few, but they are an important few to the child.

This sense of drama can turn inward as well and focus on physical symptoms. Recurring headaches or a persistent cough may lead preteens to believe that they have some dreaded disease.

This period of life is extremely intense. The highs are higher and the lows are lower than ever before. In fact, the displayed sadness of this age can bring tears to anyone's eyes. The wise parent, realizing that these intense emotions are important to express, will simply share a compassionate sigh.

Fairness. Fairness is an important issue to emerging adolescents. Their expertise in analyzing inconsistencies drives them on a continual search for justice. They are intuitively aware of "fakiness" and lies and are equally sensitive to signs of favoritism. Because of this, classroom decision making can become tedious, and I have to pull names out of a hat to determine who will run the next errand or who will speak next. And when I do make arbitrary decisions, I inevitably find myself explaining why I have allowed one student, but not another, to continue a particular activity. Still, given reasons for seemingly inconsistent decisions, children seem better able to construct moral reasoning on their own.

Parent Bonding. Another symptom of this age can be a shift in the preadolescent's primary parent relationship. Girls who formerly worked easily with their mothers on homework assignments now may seek Dad's help instead. Similarly, boys may enter into heated arguments with Dad and turn to Mom for help. Rejected parents who experience this shift as painful often find it helpful to simply recognize that it goes with the age.

Loneliness. Loneliness can become a problem at any age. The emerging adolescent often outgrows the childhood friendships that

Photo by David S. Strickler-Strix Pix

were once so rewarding. Suddenly discovering that these relationships were based on commonality of activities or on something as trivial as similar clothing style, the preadolescent begins to desire more from friendship. He is not yet sure of what he's looking for, but he knows that his old buddy Billy does not have it anymore. Children who have activities outside of school seem to bypass this predicament more easily than those who do not. These children identify themselves in one way during school hours and in another way outside of school. Since academic success does not provide great incentive to most children at this age, they need other "tags" for identification. Sports, theater groups, community activities, or after-school clubs help to provide them with some idea of who they are, as well as entertaining and stimulating them.

Parent Survival
Neither prescribed remedies nor Band-Aids can cure the preadolescent's tears and emotional injuries. However, there are a number of ways to ease parent survival during these years.

Be consistent with your preteen. Children are much more secure when boundaries are clearly set for them. If you see a need to break the rule in a particular circumstance, be sure to clearly state your reasons for why this time and not another.

Preview step-by-step the scenarios for situations that are likely to arise. "Okay, Sally, so you want to go to the movies. Where will you keep your money? How much will you need? Will you want treats, too? What if you cannot get into this feature? What then?" Help your child to walk mentally through situations and to anticipate what to do if the unexpected should occur, as it often does. Because eleven- and twelve-year-olds are becoming increasingly independent, this exercise in guidance allows them some freedom and you some peace of mind. Previewing can help in setting up baby-sitting guidelines, preparing for a trip alone on public transit, or being anywhere without adult supervision.

Let your child know how you feel. If you feel hesitant about sending your preteen to an overnight camp-out in the woods with friends, tell your child why. It is not necessary to provide the gory details of the kidnap fantasy you may have, nor should you attempt to make your own phobias a problem for your child. Simply let him or her know that even adults are often confused, frustrated, and uncertain.

My students are amazed when I mention that I, too, have arguments with my friends, and they are reassured when I describe my ways of attempting to solve these conflicts, all the while pointing out the parallels to their conflicts. Preadolescents are often shocked to find that adults can feel angry at other adults, that we cry at sad movies, are hurt by an offhand comment, or feel shy when entering a room of strangers. Too often, these young folks feel that misery seeks only them. By letting our youngsters realize that life will throw monkey wrenches from time to time, we can help them to recognize that the feelings they have are not wrong, ridiculous, or foreign to life experience.

Offer lots of examples of rational thought. When the going gets tough, your child will hang onto your words of wisdom. Discuss genetics and family history if your preadolescent is overly concerned about height or weight or shape. If everyone in your family is short, it is time to help your youngster see the writing on the wall. If your daughter is overly bothered by her lack of bosom, go through the family album together. My doctor told me that my pimples would be gone when I turned nineteen, and for six years I lived for my nineteenth birthday. My pimples were not gone by then; nevertheless, I was able to reassure myself that he could have been off by a bit, and that any day they would disappear. I *knew* there would be an end to them someday!

When I must help my students to face a difficult situation, I ask them, "What is the worst thing that could happen?" and get them to think about how they would cope with such an occurrence. Then we work back to the "next worst thing that could happen." After two or three opportunities to describe these thoughts concretely, the children are usually able to let go of their fear or frustration; they have faced the enemy and its power over them is loosened. This is especially effective with a student who is facing divorce in the household. We talk about whose house she will live in, ways of adjusting to visiting the ousted parent, and how difficult it will be on her parents, too. Tears are soon dried, and the day looks a little brighter. Rational thought is not a cure-all, but it does help in analyzing the situation. It also helps the child to begin an inner dialogue using this type of reasoning.

Always attempt to give reasons for the decisions you make. This will give your preteen insights into future problem-solving experiences.

Even if you can only come up with "because I love you and it's too scary for me," give a reason. If you do not, your emerging adolescent will invent remarkable reasons for your decisions and will base them on his or her prevailing mood and opinion of you at the moment. Provided with reasonable explanations for decisions, your child will begin to understand that adults do not pull answers out of a hat.

Talk to your child's teacher. It is best to consult the teacher as soon as you are aware of a possible problem and to provide as much detail as you can. The more a teacher knows, the more she or he can help a child during school hours. The teacher may not have the answers, but the contact will provide assurance and support to all involved.

Preteens, like teenagers, live in the middle of change. Our task as adults is a tricky one: to acknowledge the child who still needs our protection and advice while freeing the young adult to explore and experiment with his or her new world. Preteens are simultaneously tentative and bold in their approach to life.

As my sixth graders leave and go on to seventh and then eighth grade, I realize that they are facing some of the most challenging years of their lives. To help them prepare for upcoming changes, I encourage them to ask adults about difficult times in their lives. Very often the teenage years will be mentioned. Even having experienced firsthand the plight of the emerging adolescent, we find that we have no ready answers. But we do have a willingness to listen, bite our tongues, swallow our laughter, appreciate the struggle, and help them through each crisis until the sun shines through once again.

3

CHARACTER DEVELOPMENT
DURING ADOLESCENCE

Betty K. Staley

*The whole object of the universe to us is the formation of character.
If you think you came into being for the purpose of taking an important part
in the administration of events, to guard a province of the moral creation
from ruin, and that its salvation hangs on the success of your single arm,
you have wholly mistaken your business.*
—Ralph Waldo Emerson[1]

Young people in their twenties are distinguishable by their character; in other words, by the kinds of people they are. Their values,
motivations, and principles speak to older adults more clearly than do
their physical appearance, their keen intellects, or their latest posses-
sions. If we are in a position to hire a young person, we look for a
responsible individual who can be trusted to work hard and perform
tasks well. If we rent a house to a young person, we ask for character
references. If our son or daughter plans to marry, we consider the character of the intended spouse to be more important than how much
wealth or prestige he or she brings to the relationship.

In each case, we want to know whether the person can be trusted,
whether the person has courage to face his or her deeds, and whether
the person lives an ethical life. In short, we are concerned with
integrity.

The Role of Biography
Character develops slowly. In the first seven years of life, as a person
emerges from infancy to toddlerhood to childhood, that child's constitution is most noticeable. Some children are solid and compact,
while others are lanky. Some look like football players, and others like
wisps barely touching the earth. Beneath the physical surface, how-

Photo by Michael Weisbrot

ever, the child is forming a picture of who she or he is. The attitude of parents and other adults helps create the youngster's sense of self-worth. Am I respected and honored? Do my parents give me the knowledge and assurance that I am worthwhile and important? Do I feel secure within the family? Reflections on such questions form an integral part of an individual's developing character.

In the years between seven and fourteen, the child's temperament begins to emerge. The quality of our interactions with the child depends largely on his or her emotional characteristics. A child may outwardly appear choleric (aggressive), melancholic (thoughtful), phlegmatic (lethargic), or sanguine (flighty). Unconsciously, however, the child is continuing to develop a sense of identity: Am I easily pushed around? Do I stand up for myself? Do I tell the truth? Some youngsters are born with profound moral convictions that no outer force can dissuade, and they reveal such inner strength that others feel uplifted in their presence. However, most children of this age echo their parents' standards of morality.

During adolescence, constitution and temperament move into the background, and character comes to the fore. Between the ages of fourteen and twenty-one, youngsters begin to separate their beliefs from those of their parents and decide for themselves what their values are. This is the primary time for character formation. Later, between twenty-one and forty-two, individuals continue to refine their character by working consciously with their particular hereditary tendencies and cultural influences. By the time most people reach their forties, they have become "themselves."

The Role of Adults

Character expresses the essential nature of an individual. Forming its foundation are a person's moral and ethical convictions as well as his or her guiding motivations. At the same time, character evolves in the process of meeting the world; it is shaped by experiences with people and situations. Formed from within and shaped from without, character development in the teenage years occurs in response to the family, the educational setting, and the larger social and cultural atmosphere. In essence, it occurs in response to daily encounters with adults.

Although we as adults cannot "teach" character traits directly, we can influence their development. We can acknowledge a teenager's demonstration of such noble traits as loyalty, courage, compassion, honesty, commitment, steadfastness, attentiveness, fairness, and idealism. We can also share with teenagers the great religious and ethical systems of the world, which describe the force of character in many different terms: the conscience, the still small voice, the inner light, the Truth, the Spirit, the Christ force, the Holy Ghost, the Tao, and the voice of God.

Adults can help immensely by emphasizing the importance of character development—the task at hand for teenagers. As American society's respect for traditional institutions has wavered, so too has its respect for ethical values. Over the last twenty years, two extremes of "virtuous" behavior have emerged. One is a very strict code of behavior that leaves little room for an individual to disagree; the other is a "do your own thing" standard, which denies the existence of objective values and advocates that all decisions serve one's own needs. These attitudes mislead teenagers and divert them from the serious and subtle task of character development.

Parental attitudes and other adult influences throughout childhood have an important bearing on the young person's sense of security. Teenagers who feel secure in themselves are not easily swayed by others. They are able to put off immediate rewards and aim for long-range goals. These youngsters know what to do in unfamiliar situations and are able to handle challenges. Insecure teenagers have more difficulty handling new situations and making decisions that will benefit them in the long run. Because they do not feel secure within themselves, they may seek immediate rewards and require outer forms of recognition and status.

Another important role for parents and other adults is to set standards. Meeting expectations in a family, school, or organizational setting helps the adolescent cultivate ideals, aim for the "noble," and develop inner strength. When these standards are not met, the adult has the responsibility to reflect this to the teenager, however unpleasant it may be. No one likes to be told that he or she has fallen short, but such feedback does bring long-term benefits by inspiring the youngster to set a direction for his or her moral life.

All people make mistakes, and the way we as adults handle them can make a world of difference. The following examples, drawn from my own experience, reveal two different ways of responding to a teenage theft. In the first situation, a fourteen-year-old stole some flasks from a chemical company. When the teacher took the student and the flasks back to the company so that the student could make amends, they were told, "Never mind. That happens all the time." Here a valuable opportunity was lost. Instead of being encouraged to work on his character, the youngster was given the message that what he had done was common and acceptable.

The second episode occurred during a trip to New York City, after an eighth-grade class had dinner in Chinatown. As the youngsters climbed onto the school bus, they began comparing the ashtrays they had taken. The teacher marched the class back to the restaurant and had the students individually return the ashtrays and apologize. The restaurant manager expressed gratitude and explained that although it was common for school groups to take items, no teacher had ever responded in this way. The event made such a significant impact that several students mentioned it years later.

We can help young people develop character by bringing them face-to-face with themselves and helping them set things right. This communicates that objective standards of moral behavior do exist and that we expect youngsters to live up to them. It also implies that if they are not able to do so by themselves, we are available to help. In this way, we show teenagers that we care about how they live their lives, and we awaken in them a keener awareness of their own moral nature.

In some instances, teenagers need the courage of adults to help them face an unpleasant situation and develop from it. An example: two teenage girls used their lunchtime to do a "lawn job"—that is, to make deep ruts on a lawn by driving a car over it. The girls were identified, and the owner of the property worked with the school and parents to ensure that the youngsters would replant and repair the lawn. This was an effective way to have the girls pay for the damage: they felt much better afterward, having been able to set things right.

When teenagers get in trouble, they are usually calling for help—and often for parental attention. It does not help when parents close their eyes and pretend that an incident did not occur. Nor does it help to focus on protecting the youngster from punishment. Such responses are a disservice to the adolescent. Similarly, parents who respond to trouble by placing the blame on others convey a negative message about accepting responsibility for one's own actions. The important question to ask here is, how can we make the most of a troubled situation so that our youngster learns the right lessons from it?

It is wise to remember that the young person has an inner desire to live a moral life. This becomes evident when youngsters are asked to choose their own punishment: they are often much harder on themselves than one would expect. Teenagers know when what they are doing is wrong. And although they may at first respond in a hostile manner or lie about what they have done, they eventually admit to being grateful for adult intervention and for the opportunity to learn a lesson.

I remember a young man who always seemed "smooth." Although he was never caught in a misdeed, it was obvious that he was somehow involved with most behind-the-scenes activities that went on at school. When confronted, he would put on an extremely innocent look and explain how hurt he was for having been accused of lying, cheating, bullying, or whatever the situation happened to be. Nevertheless, as a teacher I continued to meet with him to discuss the problems as they arose or to call him on his antics. As he grew older, we were able to speak about difficulties with more directness. Although he never acknowledged having been wrong, he did joke about it. After graduating, he sent me a letter, saying: "First of all, I can't tell you how glad I am that you have been my adviser. I know that might sound silly, but it's true. These past four years I have learned so much from you, not just academically but about life and people. I'll never forget all the little conferences and meetings I had to go to with you. At the time, I hated them, but now I realize how much they taught me. Thank you so much for everything, and I'll always remember you."

Character develops not only by making amends for mistakes and by confronting errant behavior but also by owning up to the truth. Parents can easily encourage this practice. For example, we can praise our young child for telling the truth rather than express anger about what has occurred. Later, the child will have numerous occasions to put this message into practice. In school, for instance, he or she is likely to come face-to-face with cheating. The questions that arise lead naturally to moral decision making: Should I cheat? Will I be caught? Is it right? How do I feel about my friends cheating? The inner struggle that the adolescent undergoes in making such decisions is a character-building struggle.

Adults influence a young person's character development in several ways but perhaps most profoundly by personal example. Adults who

Photo by Lisa Law Productions

base their decisions on inner moral standards make a vivid impression. Even if adolescents find such decisions difficult to understand at the time, they will be deeply affected by the example of moral integrity.

Character-Building Opportunities

Opportunities for character development present themselves as the adolescent begins facing existential questions and dilemmas. What will my life be like? What do I want to stand for? What will I sacrifice for? The youngster decides on priorities as different values come up for consideration. Is service more important than money? If I have to go against my beliefs to work in a place, is it worth it? Do I want something enough to cheat for it? Am I being true to myself?

Making plans for the future provides a wealth of character-building opportunities. For example, a nineteen-year-old college student had always planned to work in nuclear physics and arranged her course of study with this in mind. When she discovered that most jobs for such physicists were connected with nuclear power plants or weapons manufacture, she felt she had to give up this dream and choose another major. Others planning for the future have asked themselves the following questions: Should I continue my education when I would rather get a job and buy a fancy car? Should I choose a career that serves other people or one that brings in lots of money? Should I take initiative or coast along? Should I help my family so that my younger siblings can continue their education?

Character develops as youngsters separate from adults and learn to make moral decisions on their own. It develops in freedom and cannot be imposed by another person. As young people struggle to live their own lives, they often choose values different from those of their parents and set a path contrary to all that has been given. Striking out to find one's own direction in life frequently involves struggling against enormous odds.

Despite what parents can provide, youngsters want to make it on their own. A youngster with outstanding intellectual aptitude may decide to work at a menial job to experience a particular kind of life. The hardships imposed by the work may be difficult for a parent to accept, but it is important to appreciate that, for the adolescent, inner principles have taken priority over the easy way of life. Such a decision, rooted in the individual's ego, is not the same as rebellion. It is a decision consciously made because higher values are at stake. When young people act on such impulses, it is very difficult to talk them out of their plans. They are willing to risk loss of approval, forgo financial security, and suffer isolation in the pursuit of their goals.

One father I know was looking forward to the day when his son would assume his successful business. The son decided, however, to be a teacher. A young, unmarried woman became pregnant; although her parents urged her to have an abortion, she believed it was wrong and assumed the responsibility of raising her child even though it was against her parents' wishes. A student spoke to a teacher about cheating in the classroom even though he knew he would be pressured by his classmates for having reported it. A young woman noticed that the teacher had made a mistake in scoring her test; she turned it in to be rescored even though the corrected grade would be lower.

Each of us has experienced moments that test our character, that offer us the opportunity to become better human beings or rise to greater heights. These moments may pass unheeded. We may, instead, give in to greed, or neglect to follow through on an important matter, or let down a friend. Such experiences often linger and haunt us until we are able to resolve them.

Service provides a significant opportunity for character building, and engaging in service-oriented tasks summons a teenager's idealism and goodwill. Is the youngster expected to contribute efforts to the family, or does every job come with a cash value? Does the youngster have the chance to help others in the community—perhaps an elderly person or someone with a disability? The answers to these questions may spell the difference between service as chore and service as a means of personal growth.

High school organizations offer many possibilities for leadership, especially when advisers work hard to help students develop their priorities. Here, the teenager faces such issues as handling responsibility, dealing with repercussions if the responsibility is not met, and sacrificing personal pleasures in favor of fulfilling broader needs. In the process, the individual is rewarded with the satisfaction of a job well done. Family responsibilities, jobs, and involvement in other organizations also offer opportunities to develop character.

All youngsters have special qualities, and the way they choose to use these determines who they are. Working directly with these personality traits provides challenging opportunities for moral decision making. Maintaining a balance between serving oneself and serving other people is vital. It requires adolescents to use their special talents to benefit others while avoiding egotistical or self-serving behaviors.

For example, an adolescent may be very inquisitive, interested in details about people and subjects. He or she can express this quality in an antisocial way—by gossiping maliciously or by pursuing a subject in an isolated or narrow-minded manner (as in the case of the "mad scientist" attempting to gain power). In contrast, if the youngster's inclination is to bring these talents to others, he or she can direct this curiosity toward understanding people's individual needs and behaviors. In this way, a teenager's interest in details can serve humanity.

Perhaps the adolescent has a strong sense of order and knows that when he or she is involved, things happen. If motivated by self-concern, this person may insist on deciding how things should be; disagreement from others might evoke temper tantrums, slammed doors, frustration, or feelings of being unappreciated. The teenager who is motivated to serve others, however, can transform this quality to benefit others. A strong sense of order can help a group figure out what needs to be done, and leadership skills can inspire others to act on these solutions. This quality is clearly described in the *Tao Te Ching*:

> The highest type of ruler is one of whose existence
>   the people are barely aware.
> Next comes one whom they love and praise.
> Next comes one whom they fear.
> Next comes one whom they despise and defy.
> The sage is self-effacing and scanty of words.
> When his task is accomplished
>   and things have been completed
> All the people say,
>   "We ourselves have achieved it."

Another personality trait that can serve as a curse or a blessing is flexibility. A flexible teenager may keep changing to adapt to whatever comes, regardless of the values involved. In this case, what appears as flexibility is a disguised need for peer group acceptance. When morally developed, however, flexibility can keep a process in motion and inspire an exchange of ideas. A teenager who can put this quality to work for others is able to help a group heal wounds, see new possibilities, and proceed in a creative and constructive manner. Character development does not come easily. It requires effort, time, and commitment. Although adults can support the process, the real working materials are an individual's special personality qualities. Beginning in adolescence, youngsters become conscious of these challenges and take on the work of shaping their own evolution.

Rudolf Steiner points out that there are special times in our lives when our inner voice speaks most strongly, usually in relation to our life's work. These moments occur in eighteen-and-a-half-year rhythms, at about ages nineteen, thirty-eight, and fifty-six. At these times, we face ourselves in a particularly direct way and are given an occasion to evaluate our progress and shape our future. Some people become ill, others face terrible loneliness, and still others make decisions that turn their entire lives in new directions. Whatever our response may be, our past efforts in character development come to our aid in these moments.

Developing character is the great work of human life. We become what we will ourselves to become. Whether we believe that we are inspired by spiritual beings or that we develop out of rational ethical sources, our efforts are called upon to shape, mold, and form what is truly human. This great work is begun during the adolescent years.

Notes

1. Bliss, Perry, ed. *The Heart of Emerson's Journals* (New York: Dover Publications, 1939), 39.

For More Information

Elkind, David. *All Grown Up & No Place to Go.* Reading, Mass.: Addison-Wesley Publishing Company, 1984.

Lievegoed, Bernard. *Phases of Childhood.* Hudson, N.Y.: Anthroposophic Press, 1987.

Steiner, Rudolf. *Human Values in Education.* London: Rudolf Steiner Press, 1971.

——. *Waldorf Education for Adolescence.* E. Sussex, U.K.: Kolisko Archive Publications, 1980. (Distributed by St. George Book Service, P.O. Box 225, Spring Valley, N.Y. 10977.)

4

TEENAGERS IN THE
POSTMODERN WORLD

David Elkind

Perhaps without fully realizing it, our society has moved into what can be called the postmodern era. This era is in many ways quite different from the modern period that preceded it. It has witnessed a reinvention of our conception of the family, of children, and of adolescents.

The Modern Era

The modern era in the United States began roughly with the American Revolution and intensified during the Industrial Revolution. During this time there developed an idealization of technology, of science, and of knowledge in general. It was the era of the grand theories in physics (Newton), in biology (Darwin), in history (Spengler), in economics (Marx and Engels), in sociology (Weber), and in psychiatry (Freud). Above all, the modern era was marked by the idea of progress, the idea that the world and the people in it were getting better. Both the democratic and the Communist political ideologies had human progress and betterment as their goals.

The nuclear family as we know it was a product of the modern era. With the rapid rise of industrialization and urbanization, communal and extended family life came to an end. There gradually came to be an increasing distance between the family and society at large. As sociologist Christopher Lasch described it in his book of the same title, the family became a "haven in a heartless world." The modern nuclear family provided support, nurturing, and relief from the harshness and competitiveness of the world of work and commerce. The nuclear family was dominated by the sentiments of romantic love, maternal love, and domesticity—the special relation between parents and children. Within the nuclear family, children were regarded as

Photo by Michael Weisbrot

innocent and in need of protection, while adolescents were seen as immature and in need of adult guidance and direction.

The Postmodern Era

The postmodern era had its roots in the cataclysmic events of the first half of the twentieth century: two World Wars, the Great Depression, the Holocaust, and the dropping of the first atomic bomb. A growing awareness of the degradation of the environment and the depletion of natural resources and an increasing concern about population growth have contributed to its development. The postmodern era is characterized by a new distrust of technology and science, of the view of knowledge as essentially good and beneficial, and of the idea that progress is inevitable. Kant—the chronicler of human reason—was the philosopher par excellence of modernity, while Nietzsche—the chronicler of human passions—is the forerunner of postmodernism.

Postmodernism is not nihilistic, however. Rather, it is marked by an effort at "deconstruction," at challenging the grand concepts and idealizations of the modern era and replacing them with more realistic, practical, and functional ideas. For example, the many hard-edged skyscrapers and square glass-and-steel buildings built between the 1940s and the 1960s reflected the infatuation with machines and technology characteristic of their era. Postmodern architecture is marked by pastiche, that is, an amalgam of different styles and influences. It reflects a deconstruction of the idea of modernity in buildings.

The deconstruction process is also evident in other arts. Both abstract art and photorealism are commentaries on and deconstructions of the representational thrust of modern art. In literature, the writing of Jorge Luis Borges is postmodern in its melding of fact and fiction and its active involvement of the reader in the process of invention. And in science, the concern with "chaotic" events such as the dispersion of cream in a coffee cup or the making of a snowflake marks a turn away from the search for grand, all-explaining theories and a new recognition that small events can affect larger ones.

One theme of the postmodern era of particular relevance to psychiatry and psychology is the movement away from thinking in terms of "levels." In modern biology, for example, levels are seen as genotypes and phenotypes; in physics, nuclear and atomic levels of analysis; in economics, micro- and macroeconomics; in linguistics, "surface" and "deep" structures. In psychiatry, we have the conscious and

the unconscious as well as the personal unconscious and the collective unconscious.

While the postmodern temper does not deny the value of levels
thinking, it also insists on the fact that such thinking may lead us to
overlook the richness of surface level phenomena. The late Erving
Goffman, perhaps the most gifted sociologist of his time, was concerned in his book, *The Presentation of the Self in Everyday Life*, with
what he called the "dust" of human existence: the minutiae of everyday life such as waiting in line, eating alone at a restaurant, or saying
good-bye at an airport or a railway station. In psychiatry, the concern
with family "systems" reflects a new awareness of the complexity of
surface phenomena.

The Postmodern Family

The postmodern era has been witness to the deconstruction of the
nuclear family. Certainly, the idea of the home as haven has been
challenged by recently emerging evidence of child and wife abuse.
Furthermore, while the home may have traditionally been a haven for
men, it was—as the women's movement made clear—often a prison
for women. Likewise, the stereotype of maternal love, which required
that mothers stay home and rear their young children as evidence
of their devotion and even of their femininity, has evolved into a
more elastic definition of what it means to be a woman and mother.
Similarly, the notion of romantic love, that marriage meant happy-
forever-after as soon as the ring was on the finger, has given way
to the awareness that successful marriages have to be worked at and
do not just happen as a matter of course. It is evident that some of
these changes from modern to postmodern have been beneficial.
They have revised false and outdated conceptions of the family and of
women's role within it.

Our view of children has also changed from the modern to the postmodern era. The concept of childhood innocence that characterized
the modern era and that served as justification for mothers staying
home to look after and protect their offspring has been lost. In its
place we now have the concept of the "competent" child, ready and
able to cope with all of life's vicissitudes at an early age. This shift
from viewing children as innocent to viewing them as competent did
not result from hardships or injustices deriving from the conception
of childhood innocence. Rather, the conception of childhood compe-

tence was invented to accommodate the realities of the newly fluid postmodern family. For children, the replacement of the conception of childhood innocence with one of childhood competence has had more negative than positive effects.

To be sure, children are in many ways more competent than we gave them credit for in the modern era. Even young children, for example, can be quite empathic with others. Children can master a great deal of information; they are adept at learning such skills as programming a VCR or playing computer games. Yet there are limits to what children can deal with emotionally and what they can comprehend intellectually. For example, children need a lot of emotional support when their parents separate or divorce. Younger children have difficulty comprehending complex events such as the Holocaust or diseases such as AIDS. In the postmodern era, we need to be very specific about the limitations of children's capacities to comprehend facts and feelings, as well as about their competencies.

Not surprisingly, there has also been a transformation in our conception of adolescence from the modern to the postmodern era. The modern conception of adolescence was that of immaturity. Although adolescents might be physically mature, they were, nonetheless, intellectually, socially, and emotionally immature. Thanks to this conception of adolescents as immature—a view that teenagers shared—young people were subject to, and accepting of, adult authority and guidance. This concept was also embodied in our laws: offenders below the age of sixteen were treated differently from those older, even when they had committed comparable crimes.

Just as the postmodern era did away with the conception of childhood innocence, so also it did away with the conception of adolescent immaturity. In the postmodern era, adolescents are not regarded as immature. On the contrary, they are seen as sophisticated and perhaps even more knowledgeable and savvy than their parents. We have only to compare the teens in contemporary television programs such as "The Cosby Show" or "Roseanne" with the teenagers portrayed in the sitcoms of twenty years ago such as "My Three Sons" or "The Brady Bunch" to see the change in the perception of teenagers from the modern to the postmodern era.

As in the case of children, the new conception of teenagers was invented to accommodate the new conception of the family, not because of any injustices or hardships brought about by the concep-

Photo by John Schoenwalter Photography

tion of teenage immaturity. And, as in the case of children, the conception of teenage sophistication has not been beneficial for teenagers.

While in some respects, contemporary teenagers are certainly more sophisticated than earlier generations of teenagers, they are not in others. For example, while teenagers today are more sexually active (and at an earlier age) than was true in the past, many are still woefully ignorant about the realities of getting pregnant and contracting venereal disease, and sexual myths and misinformation abound.

Likewise, while teenagers may be quite sophisticated in relation to subjects of immediate interest to them, they are often quite naive about larger issues such as politics and world events. One negative effect of early sophistication may have been to narrow the range of teenagers' interests and activities. As a consequence, the development of these adolescents may be more uneven than that of teenagers in earlier generations. They are overly sophisticated in a few areas and undersophisticated in others.

The Postmodern Adolescent

The transformation from immaturity to sophistication is evident in many different domains of adolescent behavior and experiences. Some of these are sexuality, work, schooling, and identity.

Sexuality

The shift from immaturity to sophistication in our conception of adolescents is perhaps most evident in the domain of sexuality. In the modern era, premarital sex was generally limited to engaged couples or to young men and "loose" women. Middle-class women "saved" themselves for their husbands. This reflected not only a double standard with respect to men and women but also the idea that teenagers were not sufficiently mature to handle a sexual relationship that did not involve commitment. Young people generally accepted these values and the conception of their own immaturity.

The sexual revolution of the sixties changed all of that. One part of that revolution was the so-called *Playboy* philosophy, namely, that recreational sex was okay. The *Playboy* philosophy also included the notion that middle-class girls did "it" and enjoyed doing "it." *Playboy* pictures of clean-cut, girl-next-door types in the nude and in sexually provocative poses destroyed the concept of middle-class woman as pure and inviolate.

Of course, the *Playboy* philosophy would never have been broadly accepted had it not coincided with the women's liberation movement. This movement also deconstructed the conception of the "sacred" middle-class woman. Although it approached the subject from a different angle, the women's liberation movement called not only for equality in the workplace and equal educational opportunity but also for a recognition of women's sexuality. It stated that women had a right to sexual satisfaction no less than that of men and that men needed to learn how to please women just as much as women needed to learn how to please men.

As a result of this sexual revolution, premarital sex became commonplace for middle-class men and women. Not surprisingly, this change in values was quickly appropriated by teenagers. If recreational premarital sex was okay for unmarried adults, why should it not be okay for unmarried teenagers? This value system became increasingly widespread as the children of men and women who had been sexually active prior to marriage came to maturity. Parents could hardly demand abstinence from their children when they themselves had had one or more premarital partners.

As teenagers increasingly engaged in premarital sex and apparently did not fall apart in the process, our attitudes toward teenagers and sexuality changed. We have come to regard teenagers as much more mature in matters sexual than in the past. On the surface, it would appear that teenagers have no more trouble handling recreational sex than adults do. This new, postmodern view of teenage sexual sophistication has been reflected in a number of movies for teenagers, such as *Risky Business*. It is also reflected by the introduction of sexually aggressive teenage vamps in the day and evening soap operas.

The change in the conception of teenagers from immature to sophisticated has been accepted by teenagers themselves. This is reflected in the statistics regarding teenage sexual behavior. Not surprisingly, there has been a sharp rise in the number of sexually active teenagers. In the 1960s only about 10 percent of teenage girls and 25 percent of teenage boys were sexually active. Today the figures are closer to 50 percent for girls and 65 percent for boys. However, our assumption of teenage sophistication may be overdone.

That young people may not be quite as sophisticated sexually as we might like to believe is evidenced by the high rates of teenage preg-

nancy and venereal disease. And, although the threat of AIDS and
venereal disease has affected the sexual behavior of adults, it has had
little impact on teenagers. Here is another sign that our conception of
teenage sophistication may be exaggerated. For example, while young
teenagers may appear to handle sexual activity with aplomb, follow-
up studies suggest that the younger a teenager becomes sexually
active, the more likely he or she is to encounter problems in hetero-
sexual relations as an adult. Likewise, the million or so teenage pregnancies that occur each year and the ever-rising number of unmarried teenage mothers suggest that large numbers of teenage males and
females are not handling their sexual freedom in a responsible,
"sophisticated" way.

Work

In the modern era, when most work was factory work, there was a
separation between the worker and the result of his or her labors.
Unlike the premodern craftsman, who completed whole products and
had the satisfaction of seeing them from start to finish, the factory
worker merely contributed a small part to the larger whole. As a
result, the values of work had to be portrayed in ideal rather than in
practical terms to make the system palatable to those who were a part
of it. This gave rise to the so-called work ethic: the belief that regular
work habits were critical in the formation of sound character and
good morals.

The work ethic did not extend to children and youth. The employ-
ment of children in factories and coal mines was an abuse of young
people, not a lesson in the values of work. The new humanitarian
mood of the late nineteenth and early twentieth centuries led to the
passing of child labor laws both in the United States and abroad. In
effect, the child labor laws incorporated the values of the nuclear
family; they stated implicitly that children and youth were innocent
and in need of protection. The values of work were to be reaped by
adults, not by children.

In the postmodern American world, factory labor, which had
replaced farm labor as the major occupation of the populace, has itself
been relegated to a secondary position. With automation and roboti-
zation replacing people on assembly lines, factory labor has shrunk to
a small percentage of the work force. The majority of the American
populace now work in service industries. The end result of service is

Photo by Michael Weisbrot

not a product but a satisfied customer or consumer. Yet America has never had a servant class, and in some ways the idea of serving others, whether in a fast food store, department store, or supermarket, is repugnant to the American spirit. To many, service connotes subservience and as such violates the American spirit of independence.

Accordingly, work, at least in the service industries, has lost most of its moral value. It is hard for Americans to rationalize or idealize providing good service to others or to feel that such work builds character and moral values. Not surprisingly, recent studies of teenagers who work show that work in service industries does not teach young people either good work habits or positive attitudes. Young people work to earn money to make car payments or to buy records and clothing. The work-ethic view of work as valuable in and of itself, and as a source of personal satisfaction distinct from monetary reward, has largely been lost. Furthermore, only a small proportion of adolescents contribute to the expenses of the home. This accounts for the fact that the teenage group has the largest percentage of disposable income of any age group.

In a strange way, the rise to prominence of service industries has also contributed to the conception of teenage sophistication. At least on the surface, teens now can do what adults do—hold a job. But working in a McDonald's or in a market takes little training and preparation over and above the social and/or technological skills the teenager already has. Such work can be compared to baby-sitting, which requires little in the way of preparation or training. It is not surprising, therefore, that in many ways, teenagers see such work as simply and solely a way of making money.

In the postmodern era, work has been deconstructed and is no longer regarded as automatically conferring moral values on those who engage in it. Many teenagers, as well as their parents, see themselves as too sophisticated to learn anything of value from work in a service industry. At the same time, American industry is learning the importance of service. The once rigid separation between production and marketing has been broken down. In an important recent book, *The Competitive Advantage*, Harvard Business School professor Michael Porter has argued that the competitive advantage of an industry comes from attention to satisfying the customer by tying marketing closely to production. Thus it may soon be that youth, rather than disdaining the human social values inherent in service, may have to acquire them as essential components to success in any occupation.

Schooling

The poor performance of American teenagers vis-à-vis teenagers in other countries on tests of academic achievement is a cause of great national concern. This poor academic achievement is also reflected in the decline of SAT scores, particularly verbal scores, over the last twenty years. One can view the decline of academic performance among American teenagers and the rise in rates of adolescent sexual activity as postmodern phenomena. As such, they reflect the shift from the conception of teenage immaturity to teenage sophistication.

Contemporary teenagers have grown up with the mass media. They are familiar with technology and with the larger world outside of the school. In many ways, schools, particularly high schools, have not kept pace with adolescent experience. They tend to see teenagers as sophisticated socially but still in need of traditional modes of education. In fact, just the reverse is true. Teenagers often see schools as intellectually antiquarian, as places to get grades to get into college, and not as places where they can learn much of anything of relevance to their lives.

As it exists now, the typical high school still resembles the junior high and the elementary school. The subject choices of teenagers are limited, their time periods are rigidly scheduled, and the teaching follows the same fixed lesson format as that employed in the elementary and junior high schools. There is nothing to really mark the fact that teenagers are more advanced and sophisticated learners than younger children other than the substance of their curricula. Postmodern teenagers see themselves as too sophisticated for this mode of schooling.

Truly effective educational reform, therefore, would structure the high school more along college lines. Students would go to fewer classes but have many more classes to choose from. They would be required to do a great deal of reading and writing on their own. Educational programs of this sort would speak to the teenager's sense that he or she is ready to take responsibility for his or her own learning.

At the same time, many young people today realize that they are not as socially sophisticated as they sometimes give the impression of being. They still feel the need of adult guidance and supervision in the social domain. So while high school restructuring might free young people in the academic domain, it might well give them more structure socially. This need for more adult intervention in the social lives of adolescents dovetails with the issue of identity, discussed below.

Identity

The concept of ego identity, and particularly the "identity crises" of adolescence, was an invention of the modern era. It is a direct consequence of the role of the nuclear family. As it developed in the modern era, the nuclear family came to be a protective shield that kept innocent children and youth from the dangers of the larger world. Children and youth did not need a strong sense of personal identity until they went out into that world on their own in late adolescence.

In the postmodern era, however, the family is no longer nuclear and isolated but highly permeable to outside influences. More than any other modern device, television has penetrated the insularity of the family unit. Prior to television, all images within the home were personal or family images, even those images initiated by radio. To be sure, there were the images of magazines and books, but these were owned by family members and were in that sense personal or family images. For the first time, television introduced images into the home which were not connected to the daily lives of the people who lived there.

This intrusion of the outside world into the family means that from an early age children learn about child abuse, AIDS, and substance abuse. They are exposed to environmental degradation, natural catastrophes, and human tragedies. At no other time in our history could millions of young children have simultaneously witnessed a disaster such as the explosion of the space shuttle *Challenger*. The idea, therefore, that young people need a strong sense of identity only when they leave the protected confines of the nuclear family has to be altered. Children and adolescents need a strong sense of identity if they are not to be overwhelmed by the threats and dangers of the external world to which they are exposed from an early age.

Young people can acquire the sense of self necessary to withstand this onslaught of worldly dangers and disasters by activities within the family. With all of its weaknesses, the postmodern permeable fam-

Photo by Michael Weisbrot

ily nonetheless has many strengths. If families build on these strengths, they can provide children with the psychological capital they need to meet the demands of a harsh world. These three family strengths might be called the "three C's": the sense of continuity, the sense of connectedness, and the sense of confirmation.

Young people acquire a sense of personal continuity through the telling and retelling of family stories and through talk and reflections on the growth and development of family members. They acquire a sense of connectedness through learning the complex and unique set of family habits and rituals that deal with issues such as gift giving, illness, and celebrations. Such habits of the home unite family members but also provide tools for adaptation to the larger society. Finally, young people acquire a sense of confirmation through playing many diverse family roles, through the use of family names, and by living in and sharing a family home.

In the postmodern era, therefore, teenagers do not need to break with the family to attain a sense of personal identity. They have been forging a sense of personal identity and dealing with the external world from an early age. This is a healthy adaptive reaction to the realities of the postmodern world and may explain why teenagers today seem to feel less pressure to break from the home than was true in the past. Many young people are taking longer to finish college, and many are living with their parents after graduating.

While in part this pattern reflects postmodern economics, it also reflects a greater continuity in family life than was true during the modern era. During that time, men in particular were expected to leave home and prove their masculine self-sufficiency and independence when they reached a certain age. This rupturing of family ties was often necessary because the nuclear family had been too tight and confining. In the permeable family, ties are not so close and do not have to be broken as completely as was necessary in the past. When children experience a sense of mutuality in the family from an early age, they can maintain this mutuality in an unbroken way once they reach young adulthood.

This "new look" in postmodern family life has created some interesting reversals. In the modern era, it was often the teenager who wanted to break away from the family and the family who resisted. Mothers who had devoted themselves to their children saw little purpose in their lives once those children left the nest. But in today's world, parents spend only one-quarter to one-third of their lives in parenting. They recognize and look forward to a life after their children are grown. It is now often the parents who are happy to see the young people off on their own and the young people who would like to continue their life as family members. The permeable family is more continuous than the nuclear family, and that is one of its strengths.

Conceptions of childhood and adolescence, no less than those of the family and of parents, are social inventions that serve the social, political, economic, and psychological needs of people at a given time in history. The modern era needed a nuclear family, idealized mothers replete with maternal love, and innocent children and immature teenagers. The postmodern, permeable family requires parents who care for themselves as well as others, children who are competent, and teenagers who are sophisticated.

These new conceptions of family, of parents, and of children and youth require new responses from education and from the helping professions. Although the conception of teenage sophistication has some negative consequences, it is a reality. In our dealings with youth, we have to understand that they view themselves as equal to us in the ways of the world. Our real task is finding ways to respect this sense of sophistication while providing the moral support and guidance that many young people still look to the older generation to provide.

Are the postmodern, permeable family, competent child, and sophisticated teenager better or worse than the nuclear family, the innocent child, and the immature teenager? As suggested earlier, a basic tenet of postmodernism is that change is not necessarily progress and that questions have to be dealt with in specifics rather than in sweeping generalities. The permeable family is certainly better for women than the nuclear family, but at least at present it is not as good an environment for children and teenagers. Once we have reconciled our conceptions of children and adolescents to their real abilities and limitations, some of the postmodern pressures on them will ease.

Hermann Hesse wrote in his novel, *Siddhartha*, that every society and every age has its joys and its tragedies, its strengths and weaknesses. The worst times for young people, however, are the transition periods between one social era and another. We are living in such an era. Children and youth blossom in times of constancy, not change. They need a secure, reliable world in which to grow. They do not have it now, as we move from the modern to the postmodern world. The dismaying increase in problem behavior among children and youth is ample evidence in support of this observation. Hopefully, as we become established in the postmodern way of life, children and youth will once again find the constancy of values, standards, and beliefs that makes growing up a joy as well as a chore. We are just not there yet.

PART II:
ISSUES AND PROBLEMS

Photo by Michael Weisbrot

THE CHANGES OF PUBERTY

Talking to Teens About What's
Happening to Their Bodies

Lynda Madaras

It was one of those perfectly languid summer days when the heat is so rich and thick you can taste the scent of summer wildflowers in the air. My eight-year-old daughter and I were slowly making our way downstream through the woods by our house. It was one of those magic moments that sometimes happen between mothers and daughters. All the years of diaper changing, complicated child-care arrangements, hectic juggling of career and motherhood, nagging about bedrooms that need cleaning and pets that need feeding, all the inevitable resentments, conflicts, and quarrels seemed to fade away, leaving just the two of us, close and connected.

We stopped to sun ourselves on a rock, and my daughter shyly told me she had some new hairs growing on her body.

"Right down there," she pointed.

I was filled with pride as I watched her scrambling among the rocks, a young colt, long-limbed and elegant and very beautiful. I marveled at her assurance and ease. Her transition into womanhood would be so much more graceful than my own halting, jerky, and sometimes painful progress through puberty.

I was also proud of our relationship, proud that she felt comfortable enough to confide in me. Never in my wildest imaginings would I have thought of telling my mother that I'd discovered pubic hairs growing on my body. It was simply not something we could have discussed. I was glad that it was going to be different between my daughter and me.

We didn't talk much more about her discovery that day. Weeks and months passed without further mention of the topic, but our relationship remained close and easy.

"Enjoy it while you can," my friends with older daughters would tell

Photo by Marilyn Nolt

me, "because once they hit puberty, it's all over. That's when they really get an attitude. There's just no talking to them." I listened in smug silence. I knew the stereotype: the sullen, sulky adolescent daughter and the nagging harpy of a mother who can't communicate with each other. It was going to be different for us.

My daughter must have been nine or ten when it started—her first taste of the nasty world of playground politics and the cruel games young girls play with each other. She'd arrive home from school in tears; her former best friend was now someone else's best friend; she'd been excluded from the upcoming slumber party or was the victim of some other calculated schoolgirl snub. She'd cry her eyes out. I didn't know what to say.

"Well, if they're going to be like that, find someone else to play with," I'd say.

The tears flowed on. They got to be a weekly, then a twice-weekly event. This went on for months and months. And then I finally began to realize that no sooner had she dried her tears than she was on the telephone, maliciously gossiping about some other little girl, a former friend, and cementing a new friendship by plotting to exclude this other girl. I was indignant, and I began to point out the incon-sistency in her behavior.

"You don't understand," she'd yell, stomping off to her bedroom and slamming the door.

She was right; I didn't understand. From time to time, I'd talk to the other mothers. It was the same with all of us. Why were our daughters acting like this? None of us had any answers.

"Well, girls will be girls," signed one mother philosophically. "They all do it, and we did the same when we were their age."

I reached back over the years, trying to remember. Were we really that horrible? Then I remembered the Powder Puffs, a club my girl friends and I belonged to. Unlike the Girl Scouts and the other adult-sanctioned after-school clubs, the Powder Puffs had no formal meet-ings and no ostensible purpose—which is not to say that the club didn't have a purpose. It did. The membership cards, which were wondrously official-looking since one girl's father had run them off in his print shop and which we carried around in the cloudy cellophane inserts of our identical genuine vinyl-leather wallets, certified us as members of this all-important Group. As if that weren't identification enough, we moved around in an inseparable herd, ate lunch together in our special territory of the playground, sat together giggling like a gaggle of geese in school assemblies, wrote each other's names on the canvas of our scuffed tennis shoes, combed our hair the same way, dressed alike, and generally made life miserable for the girls who were not members of our group.

Today, some twenty years later, I can only vaguely recall the names and faces of the other members of the Powder Puffs. I do, however, remember one girl so vividly that I can almost count the freckles on her face. Her name was Pam, and she was most emphatically not a member of the group, although she wanted desperately to be—so desperately, in fact, that she took to writing notes that she'd leave in my desk:

> Dear Lynda,
> Please, Please, Please let me join the Powder Puffs.
> If you say I'm OK, the rest of the girls will too.
> Please!!! Please!!! Please!!! Please, please, please!
>
> Pam

The notes embarrassed me horribly, and, of course, the mere act of writing them doomed Pam forever to the status of outsider. I have conveniently forgotten how Pam fared after that. I know she never got to be a Powder Puff, and I imagine we made her life even more miserable with snickers and snubs, behind-the-back whisperings, and the usual sorts of adolescent tactics.

At any rate, what's really frightening is that I wasn't any crueler than most adolescent girls. I talk to other women about their relationships with other girls during those years and hear the same sorts of stories. The milk of human kindness does not flow freely in the veins of pubescent girls. Maybe, I thought, the mother who sighed that business about "girls being girls" was right. We all did it, and now our daughters were playing the same games, by the same rules. Maybe it was inevitable. Maybe it was just the nature of the beast. I didn't like this idea, but there it was.

To add to the things I didn't like, there was a growing tension between my daughter and me. She was terribly moody, and it seemed as if she was always angry with me. And I was often angry with her. Of course, we'd always quarreled, but now the quarrels were almost constant. The volume of our communications reached a new decibel level. There was an ever-present strain between us.

All of this bothered me a great deal, but what was even more disturbing was the change in her attitude about her body. In contrast to the shy wonder that greeted her first pubic hairs, there was now a complete horror at the idea of developing breasts and having her first period. Like most "modern" mothers, I wanted my daughter's transition from childhood to womanhood to be a comfortable, even joyous, time. I had intended to provide her with all the necessary information in a frank, straightforward manner. This, or so went my reasoning, would eliminate any problems.

But here was my daughter telling me she didn't want to grow breasts or have her first period. I asked why but didn't get much further than "because I donwanna." I countered with an it's-great-to-grow-up pep talk that rang hollow even to my own ears.

Clearly something was amiss. I thought I'd made all the necessary information available in the most thoroughly modern manner. But the anticipated results, a healthy and positive attitude toward her body, had not materialized.

I thought long and hard about all of this, and finally I began to realize that I hadn't given my daughter all the information I thought I had. Although she was amazingly well informed about the most minute details of ovum and sperm, pregnancy and birth, the physical details of intercourse, and even the emotional content of love-making, she knew nothing, or next to nothing, about menstruation and the changes that would take place in her body over the next few years. She'd seen me in the bathroom changing a tampon, and I'd tossed off a quick explanation of menstrual periods, but I'd never really sat down and discussed the topic with her. I'd read her any number of marvelous children's books that explain conception, birth, and sexuality, but I'd never read her one about menstruation. Obviously, it was time to do that.

So, full of purpose, I trotted off to the library and discovered that no such book existed. The more deeply I researched the topic, the less surprised I was at this fact.[1] Throughout history, in culture after culture, menstruation has been a taboo subject. The taboo has taken many forms: one must not eat the food cooked by a menstruating woman, touch objects she has touched, look into her eyes, or have sex with her. We no longer believe that the glance of a menstruating woman will wither a field of crops, that her touch will poison the water in the well, or that having sex with her will make a man's penis fall off, but the menstrual taboo is, nonetheless, alive and well.

Of course, we are no longer banished to menstrual huts each month, as were our ancestral mothers in more primitive societies. But as Nancy Friday argues in *My Mother, My Self*, our release from monthly exile does not necessarily represent a more enlightened view of menstruation. Rather, Friday says, thanks to centuries of conditioning, we have so completely internalized the menstrual taboo that it's simply not necessary to bother any longer with menstrual huts. Our modern tribe needn't go to such lengths to remove any disturbing sight or mention of menstruation from its collective consciousness. We do it ourselves, through our ladylike avoidance of any public discussion of the topic and our meticulous toilet-paper mummification of our bloodied pads and tampons.

So total is our silence that we ourselves are sometimes not aware of it. "Oh, yes," the mother says, "I told my daughter all about it." "My mother never told me anything," the daughter says.

Even if we are conscious of this silence and decide that it is time that this deplorable situation was dealt with, the taboos and our cultural embarrassment about menstruation may still take their toll. Wanting our daughters to have a positive view of their natural bodily functions, particularly if we have suffered in this area, we summon up our courage and carefully rehearse the proper lines. Intent on improving the script our mothers wrote for us, we boldly announce to our daughters: "Menstruation Is a Wonderful Part of Being a Woman, a Unique Ability of Which You Should Be Proud."

At the same time, while none of us would think of hiding our toothbrushes under the sink or in the back corners of the bathroom cupboard, it is rare to find a box of sanitary napkins prominently displayed next to the deodorants, toothpastes, and hair sprays that line the bathroom shelves of most homes. Thus, we constantly contradict our brave words and send our daughters double messages. We say it's fine and wonderful, but our unconscious actions indicate just the opposite. And as we all know, actions speak louder than words.

The sad truth is that most of us have very little in the way of positive images to offer our daughters. Indeed, most of us are remarkably ignorant of even the basic facts about our bodies and our menstrual cycle.

As a result of the research I was doing for a women's health care book, I was learning quite a bit about the physiological processes of menstruation. I could at least give a coherent explanation to a sixth

grader, but I was also learning that I had a whole host of negative attitudes about menstruation in the back of my mind, attitudes that I
had not even been conscious of before. These attitudes were changing, but who knew what else might still be lurking in the dark cor-
ridors of my subconscious? If I talked to my daughter about menstruation, I could say the right words, but would my body language, my
tone of voice (and all those other unconscious ways of communicating) betray my intended message?

I worried about all of this for entirely too long a time, until the obvious solution came to me. I simply explained to my daughter that
when I was growing up, people thought of menstruation as something
unclean and unmentionable. Now that I was older and more grown
up, my attitudes were changing. But some of the feelings I had were
old ones that I had lived with a long time, all my life in fact, and they
were hard to shake off. Sometimes they still got in my way without my
even knowing it. This, of course, made perfect sense to my daughter,
and from this starting point, we began to learn about our bodies
together.

We didn't sit down and have The Talk. My mother sat me down one
day to have The Talk, and I suppose she must have explained things
in a comprehensive way, but all I remember was my mother being
horribly nervous and saying a lot of things about babies and blood
and that when It happened to me, I could go to the bottom drawer of
her dresser and get some napkins. I wondered why she was keeping
the napkins in a dresser drawer instead of in the kitchen cabinet
where she usually kept them, but my mother was acting so weird that
I didn't want to ask questions. I just wanted to get out of there!

Having one purposeful, nervous discussion didn't seem like it would
fill the bill. Puberty is a complicated topic and it takes more than one
talk. I decided just to keep the topic in mind and bring it up now and
again. It turned out to be a pretty natural thing to do since I was
doing so much research on the female body. In one of the medical
texts I was plodding through, there was a section on puberty that discussed the five stages of pubic hair and breast development, complete
with photos. I read the section to my daughter, translating from
medicalese into English, so she would know when and how these
changes would happen in her body.

I talked to her about what I was learning about the workings of the
menstrual cycle. I showed her some magnificent pictures taken inside

a woman's body at the very moment of ovulation as the delicate, fin-
gerlike projections on the end of the fallopian tubes were reaching out
to grasp the ripe egg. A friend's mother gave us a wonderful collection
of booklets from a sanitary napkin manufacturer that dated back over
a period of thirty years. We read them together, laughing at the old-
fashioned attitudes, attitudes I'd grown up with.

In the course of our reading, we learned that most girls begin to
have a slight vaginal discharge a year or two prior to menstruation. I
had told my daughter that when she started to menstruate, I would
give her the opal ring that I always wore on my left hand, and that
she, in turn, could pass it on to her daughter one day. But when she
discovered the first signs of vaginal discharge, we were both so elated
that I gave her the opal ring on the spot. (She got a matching one
when she had her first menstrual period.)

A few hours later, as I sat working at my typewriter, I heard my
daughter yelling to me from the bathroom, "Hey, Mom, guess what I
got twenty-one of?"

We had a pregnant cat at the time and, for a few horrible moments,
I was struck numb with the thought of twenty-one kittens. But it
wasn't kittens. My daughter was back to counting pubic hairs.

The time that we'd spent learning about menstruation and puberty
had paid off. My daughter had regained her sense of excitement about
the changes that were taking place in her body. This healthy attitude
toward her body alone made our discussions worthwhile, but there
were also other changes. First of all, things between the two of us got
much better. We were back to our old, easy footing. She didn't magically start cleaning her bedroom or anything like that. We still had
our quarrels, but they subsided to a livable level. And when we
fought, at least we were fighting about the things we said we were
fighting about. The underlying resentment and tension that had been
erupting from beneath even our mildest disagreements, engulfing us
in volcanic arguments, was gone.

But the most amazing change, perhaps because it was so unexpected, was that my daughter's role in the playground machinations
began to change. In *My Mother, My Self*, Friday suggests a mother's
failure to deal with her daughter's dawning sexuality, her silence
about menstruation and the changes in the daughter's body, is perceived by the daughter as a rejection of the daughter's feminine and
sexual self.

Photo by John Schoenwalter Photography

This silent rejection of these essential elements of self, coming as it does just at the time in the daughter's life when these very aspects of femininity and sexuality are manifesting themselves in the physical changes of her body, is nothing short of devastating. The daughter feels an overwhelming sense of rejection from the figure in her life with whom she is most intensely identified. One of the ways in which the daughter seeks to cope, to gain some control over her emotional life, is through the psychodramas of rejection that she continually reenacts with her peers.

Perhaps these dramas of rejection are more along the lines of the pecking-order behavior we see among chickens. The largest, boldest chicken pecks another smaller one away from the feed dish, that chicken retaliates by pecking on another smaller and more vulnerable chicken, and so on down the line. We cannot deal with mother's rejection directly by confronting her. We are too small, too vulnerable, too defenseless; so, in a classic case of displaced aggression, we turn around and attack another little girl. Or perhaps just the opportunity to act out rejection provides some measure of relief.

Whatever the particular mechanism, I can't help but suspect that the cultural taboo about menstruation, a mother's ignorance of and reluctance to deal with the topic, and the phenomena of playground politics are inextricably tied up with one another.

One morning, sometime after my daughter and I had begun to return to our old footing, I was driving her to school when she started to talk about the problems she was having with her friends. I held my breath. This topic had become so volatile that I hadn't even broached it in months. I didn't want to say the wrong thing.

"I don't know what to do, Mommy," she told me. "I want to be Susan's and Tanya's friend, but they're always whispering and talking about Kathy, and they do it loud enough so she can hear. And I'm with them, but I really like Kathy, too."

"Well, can't you be friends with everybody?" I said, biting my tongue almost as soon as I said it. This had been one of my stock replies whenever we had talked about the subject. It usually caused a storm, but this time she merely answered me, "But if I don't get down on Kathy with them, Susan and Tanya won't be friends with me."

"So what do you do when that happens? How do you handle it?" I asked, trying to say something neutral.

"Well, I just kind of stand there. I don't actually say bad things about Kathy, but I'm there with Susan and Tanya, so it's like I'm against Kathy, too. And it makes me feel terrible, like I'm not a very good person," she said, starting to cry. "I don't know what to do."

"Well, look," I said, "Susan and Tanya are both really nice girls. Why don't you just go up to them and say 'Look, I have a problem and it's really making me feel lousy,' and then just tell them what you told me—that you want to be their friend, but you don't dislike Kathy and it makes you feel lousy if you join in putting her down."

My daughter gave me a look that told me what she thought of my suggestion.

"Not such a good idea, huh?" I offered.

"No, Mom," she agreed, and I kissed her good-bye as the school bell rang. Maybe my advice wasn't much help. Maybe it wasn't even very good advice, but at least we'd talked about the subject with each other.

Two days later, when I picked her up from school, she told me, "Well, I tried doing what you said to do."

"How did it work?"

"It worked. Susan and Tanya said that it was okay, that they'd still be friends with me even if I didn't hate Kathy."

Big of them, I thought to myself, but I didn't say anything. In truth, I was pleased; my daughter had begun to carve out a new role in the game for herself.

Perhaps Nancy Friday was right. Maybe my daughter perceived my attention to the changes taking place in her body as an acceptance of her sexual self, and this, in turn, lessened her need to participate in these playground psychodramas of rejection. I didn't know, and still don't, whether Friday's theories are real explanations, but my experiences with my own daughter certainly seemed to validate her ideas. Still, I wouldn't want to go so far as to promise you that spending time teaching your daughter about menstruation and the other physical changes of puberty will magically deliver her from the psychodramatics of puberty or will automatically erase the tensions that so often exist between parents and their adolescent daughters. But my experiences with my own daughter and, more recently, as the teacher of a class on puberty and sexuality for teens and preteens have convinced me that kids of this age need and want information about what is happening to them at this point in their lives.

Some tips on how best to go about talking with your daughter about puberty are probably in order here. First of all, be aware of the fact that you may have to initiate these conversations. As parents, we usually subject our kids to a constant stream of information and advice about virtually every aspect of their lives, from why they need to get a good education to what they should eat. But when it comes to anything having to do with sexuality, there's much less information and advice, perhaps even total silence. Our reticence or silence sends a message: It is not okay to talk about this topic. If this has been the case with you and your daughter, you'll have to put some effort into breaking this silence.

Second, remember that just one talk about puberty, or even a few, is not sufficient. Count the number of times in the last two weeks that you've discussed money, homework, irresponsibility, household chores, or another such topic with your daughter. Then count the number of times you've had a conversation about the physical or emotional changes of puberty and compare the scores. If you're batting zero, you need to work on improving your average.

Yet another piece of advice: use a casual, spur-of-the-moment approach, rather than having formal, sit-down, now-we're-going-to-discuss-puberty talks. Remember, too, that if any or all of these subjects is embarrassing for you, that's perfectly fine. Nowhere is it written, Thou shall not be embarrassed when discussing sexual topics with thine offspring. Most parents are embarrassed, especially when it comes to topics like masturbation. You can simply say something like, "Gee, this is so embarrassing for me, I can hardly talk about it. But I wished my parents had talked more to me and I don't want to let my embarrassment keep me from talking to you."

One more bit of wisdom: avoid the direct, head-on approach. Saying things like, "Would you like to talk about the changes happening in your body?" puts your daughter on the spot and probably won't work too well. Instead, take a slightly different tack. Pick an opportune moment and say something like, "When I was your age, I _____ ," and then fill in the blank with "started sprouting pubic hair and was worried because. . . ," "began developing breasts and felt. . . ," or with some misconception or embarrassing moment you had during adolescence. This is an almost surefire approach.

By virtue of your revelations about your own feelings or whatever dumb, embarrassing story you've told about yourself, you've let your daughter know (1) that it is possible to survive puberty and even to

laugh about it eventually; (2) that it's okay to be less-than-perfectly-
all-knowing-and-confident about this whole business of puberty; and
(3) that you, too, were young once—a fact that rarely impinges on
most youngsters' minds.

Adolescent boys face many of the same problems as girls; they also
have problems of their own. This culture poses some rather tricky
problems for young boys trying to find their way into manhood. On
the one hand, they have a tender, caring side; on the other, they are
confronted with all these thrilling and titillating images of a conquer-
ing, tough-guy male sexuality, which don't seem to allow much room
for being tender or caring. It must be very hard for a boy to sort all
this out, and this undoubtedly accounts for a large portion of the
adolescent male angst. Of course, what I'm talking about here isn't
any great revelation. We all know that during childhood, boys generally are allowed some room, given some social permission, to demonstrate or act out their tender side. And we all know that at adolescence they begin to move into the strange world of male adulthood in
which "real men" are not noted for their tenderness, "real men" don't
cry or ever feel uncertain about who they are or what they're supposed to do, "real men" always know the right sexual moves to make,
and "real men" are always knowledgeable and supremely confident
about sex and life in general.

To top it all off, just as they're moving from childhood into this confusing world of manhood, all these strange changes start happening to
their bodies. And chances are that nobody around them is willing to
explain these changes in any but the most cursory way, if at all. In
fact, the message that boys are getting is that somehow they're supposed to *know* about these things, for one of the main tenets of the
male mystique is that guys, or at least "real men," automatically know
everything about anything that has to do with sex.

In recent years, there's been a great deal of heated public debate
about the nature of sex education in our nation's schools, much of it
generated by conservative parents who feel that sex education belongs
in the home and that the sexual morality implied in these classes is
not up to snuff. More liberal parents have taken up the banner in
response to these attacks and have loudly and ferociously defended
sex-education programs. You may be a conservative or you may be a
liberal. You may be on one side or the other of this debate. Being a
sex-education teacher, I have my own, rather predictable, point of

Photo by Michael Weisbrot

view on the issue. But I'm willing to concede that there are valid points to be made on each side.

In general, I think that public debate on an issue like this is a good thing. I do worry, though, that it leaves parents with the impression that there is, in fact, something to debate about; that there *are* sex-education programs throughout our nation's schools. Unfortunately, this is not the case. According to one recent survey, fewer than 15 percent of the teenagers in this country are exposed to a comprehensive sex-education program. If you've been assuming, as many parents do, especially in the wake of all this debate, that at school your child is getting the information he or she needs about the sexual changes of puberty, chances are you're wrong. In most schools, sex education still consists of the kind of thing that happened when we were kids. One day, usually in the sixth grade, all the boys are mysteriously sent out to the playground for an extra "free" period, to play baseball or whatever sport is in season. The girls are herded into the auditorium and shown a film, generally produced by one of the sanitary napkin and tampon manufacturers, in which butterflies flitter through uteri and in which menstruation and the need to use these various menstrual products are explained.

The schools simply aren't doing the job we parents, for better or worse, imagine that they're doing. For the average boy, home isn't much of a source of information either. Most of the girls in my classes have been the recipients of at least one rather nervous and embarrassed "talk" from their parents (as a rule, their mothers) about menstruation, the hallmark of female puberty. But there are very few boys in my classes whose parents (either the mother or the father) have talked with them about ejaculation, the hallmark of male puberty, or about spontaneous erections, masturbation, wet dreams, or any of the other physical realities of male puberty. I'm not sure why we have decided that it's important to talk to our daughters about puberty but not so important to talk to our sons. Perhaps it has something to do with the fact that our daughter's first menstruation requires at least some sort of minimal parental response—someone's got to buy her a box of sanitary napkins or tampons and tell her how they're used and not to flush them down the toilet. When a boy ejaculates for the first time, we don't have to rush out to the store for anything, and we don't have to worry about him clogging up the plumbing. It's a lot easier to ignore our sons' "coming of age" than it is to ignore our daughters'.

Or perhaps it has to do with the fact that once our daughters begin to menstruate regularly, they become, for the first time, capable of getting pregnant. This fact alone seems to convince many parents that their daughters deserve some sex education. And yet, girls don't get pregnant by themselves. As my mother use to say, "It takes two to tango," although she was never talking about dancing when she said this.

Or maybe it's just the old male mystique, the belief that boys automatically know everything they need to know about sex. Few parents would actually argue that boys will magically understand what's happening to their bodies without someone telling them. But many parents have the attitude that puberty isn't really a "big deal" for boys. There's a popular idea in our culture that it's only girls who are embarrassed, anxious, and worried about the physical changes of puberty.

You couldn't prove it by me. In my sex-education classes, we play a game called Everything You Ever Wanted to Know about Sex and Puberty But Were Too Embarrassed to Ask, which involves a locked question box to which kids can anonymously submit questions. Judging from the questions that come up, boys are just as curious as girls about what's happening to their bodies. For every question about menstrual periods or developing breasts, there's one about wet dreams, ejaculations, or hair growth, things like, "How much of that white stuff comes out when a guy comes?" and "When will I grow a beard and start to look like my dad?" Here's one that I got earlier this year: "I am growing a mustash. Not a big mustash, but tiny hares. How can a boy by the age of eleven? He didn't have puberty yet."

The spelling and syntax are unusual, but the spirit behind the question isn't. This boy was worried about the fact that he was developing some fine hairs on his upper lip but he'd never "had puberty," by which he meant that he hadn't ever ejaculated. Generally, facial hair doesn't appear until the sex organs have started to develop and a boy has begun making sperm in his testicles and has already begun to ejaculate. But boys develop in different ways, and although it's *unusual* to develop a mustache before these other changes have begun to occur, it's certainly not *abnormal*. This boy, like most young boys, was simply looking for reassurance that what was happening to him was completely normal. It seems little enough to ask.

One reason why parents don't talk to their sons about puberty is undoubtedly simple ignorance. Most fathers didn't get much information from their own fathers. They don't exactly have a storehouse of knowledge to pass on to their sons. Although they have a general idea of what happens during puberty, having gone through it themselves, it's a rare father who can explain to his son exactly why he might have wet dreams or tell him the average age at which a boy first ejaculates. Mothers are at even more of a loss in this respect. They might feel confident enough to make a stab at telling a daughter about menstruation; after all, they've been menstruating themselves for most of their lives. But when it comes to spontaneous erections, wet dreams, and such, they're generally completely at sea.

Another factor in most parents' failure to tell their sons about the body changes of puberty is embarrassment. Sexuality is a difficult, even nigh on to impossible topic for many parents. Even those of us who feel fairly easy about discussing sex may find that there are certain areas of sexuality that we're not entirely comfortable talking over with our children. Take masturbation, for example. It's pretty difficult to discuss puberty with a boy without talking about masturbation; more than 90 percent of boys masturbate during puberty. Yet masturbation is a delicate subject, and most of us are bound to feel a little embarrassed discussing it. For one thing, how in the world do you even broach the subject in the first place? What do you say? "Hi, son, been masturbating lately?"

Talking to boys about sex is much like talking to girls. Avoid having one all-purposeful "talk." It won't cut the mustard, no matter how hard you try. It's also better to approach things casually, bringing up the topic from time to time when it seems natural to do so.

And if talking about puberty and sexuality is difficult or embarrassing for you, say so. There's nothing wrong with telling your child, "This is really embarrassing for me. . .," or "My parents never talked to me about this stuff, so I feel kind of weird trying to talk to you. . .," or whatever. Your child is going to pick up on your embarrassment anyway. By trying to pretend you're not uncomfortable, you'll only succeed in confusing your child. Once you've admitted your feelings, you've cleared the air. Your child may adopt a maddeningly smug attitude or be patronizingly sympathetic about your embarrassment, but in the end this is preferable to having him think that there is something weird about the topic itself, and it's not quite right to talk about it.

At this point I must say something about the question that parents most often ask: At what age should you tell your kids about these things? Conventional wisdom holds that you wait until the kids start asking questions. Like many bits of conventional wisdom, this strikes me as a piece of utter nonsense. We don't wait until our kids ask before we teach them how to cross the street safely. Or, if we're religious people, we don't wait until they ask about God before we give them religious instruction. Nor should we wait until they ask before we talk to them about puberty and sex. For one thing, we might end up waiting forever. Kids, having been the recipients of endless unsolicited parental guidance about virtually everything else in their lives, are not very likely to come asking questions about the one area we've been so studiously avoiding. The very fact of our silence on the topic of sexuality sends our kids the message that this is something that it's not okay to talk about.

To my mind, sex education should begin when our children are toddlers. This is not to suggest that you should provide your three-year-old with a sex manual describing sixty-eight different positions for intercourse or bog down young minds with a detailed explanation of the hormones that initiate and regulate puberty. But once your child reaches bedtime-story stage, it seems altogether appropriate to introduce the topics of conception, birth, sexuality, and puberty by means of any of the many fine children's picture books that deal with these topics.

An important distinction needs to be made here. Elementary school children and seventh graders don't need *sex* education, they need *puberty* education. Kids of this age have a multitude of questions and fears about the changes that are, or soon will be, taking place in their bodies. I get hundreds and hundreds of letters from kids, the envelopes covered with underscored pleas—"Help!" "URGENT!" "Open At Once!" "Please! Please! Write Back Right Away!!!"—and inside there are five-page letters with intricate diagrams and lengthy explanations of some lump or bump or imagined physical abnormality that has the poor kid worried sick. These children need reassuring puberty education before they're ready for sex education.

When parents and schools ignore puberty education, which addresses the true agendas of children, in favor of sex education, which is more apt to address the agendas of nervous adults, they are, in my opinion, missing the proverbial boat. Kids who aren't given reassuring puberty education when they need it do not respond as well to their parents' or schools' efforts to impart moral codes or even just safe, sane guidelines for sexual conduct.

I think it works something like this: Kids figure, "You were too embarrassed, too busy, too hung up on your own anxiety about my possible sexual activity to respond to my needs for information and reassurance about my changing body. Now, here you are, all freaked out about what I might be doing, trying to push your moral rules and sexual do's and don't's at me. Well, you're too late. My sexuality is no longer any business of yours. I'm not going to listen to a word you say. So there."

When kids are given puberty education, however, the dynamic is altogether different. It's been my experience that kids are enormously grateful for the reassurance they get from such education. I actually have had classes where kids burst into spontaneous applause when I walked into the room. I also have a file drawer full of touching letters from readers thanking me for having allayed some fear or doubt of theirs. Not only are kids grateful when their needs for reassurance are met in this way but they also develop a profound respect for and trust in the source of that reassurance.

Parents need to realize they can forge a very powerful bond with their children if they are there for them during puberty. And the ensuing trust and respect will serve all concerned when it comes to later efforts at sex education.

Notes
1. Since my daughter's adolescence, some excellent books have been published. One is *Period* by Joann Gardner-Lovlan, Bonnie Lopez, and Maria Quackenbush (San Francisco: Volcano Press, 1981).

6

ELLE AT FOURTEEN

Marion Cohen

I call her from the restaurant.
There are tears in her voice so I rush home.
Nobody ever calls her. Liza's always out and then
    never calls back, Kathy's sick, Lora's out
    with Zoe, Allison's out with Gidget and no one
    ever asks her.
In vain do I point out, "That phone was ringing for
    you all day yesterday."
("Well, not today," she sobs.)
In the bedroom she continues, "I wish I liked
    writing like you, Ma. 'Cause I don't wanna
    forget how I'm feeling right now. Could you get
    me a tape for my tape recorder?"
"I have one upstairs," I say and bring it down, then
    discreetly leave the room.
Fifteen minutes later I kneel at her keyhole.
    The low confidential tone tells me I'd better
    not creak open the door and ruin her tape.
    I'll wait awhile.
Half an hour and she's still at it—low, steady
    monotone—
Another half hour and I think, "But it's only an
    hour tape."
Quietly easing open the door I perceive the
    truth in all its glory:
She's not talking into the tape recorder. She's
    talking on the phone.

Photo by Marilyn Nolt

7

SEXUALITY EDUCATION
WITH ADOLESCENTS

Ruth Lampert

A current popular expression is, "What goes around comes around." This phrase applies especially well to the issue of sexuality in our society. I remember a telling incident in my own girlhood, over half a century ago, when my mother explained menstruation to me. She had many of the facts wrong, but I have to give her credit for having discussed the subject with me at all. She concluded by warning me that this was a very, very private matter and that I was not to talk about it with my girlfriends.

I could hardly wait to run next door and share this fascinating information with my friend Virgie. Her response surprised me and to this day saddens me. She said, "So that's why I've been bleeding down there. I was afraid to tell anyone about it. I've been stealing rags from the cleaning closet and burning them in the furnace. I thought there was something dirty about me that made this happen, and I knew I'd get whipped if I told."

What Goes Around
Many of the common beliefs and rituals of those days inhibited the enjoyment of emerging adolescent sexuality. One so-called fact was that girls did not masturbate. In fact, girls did, but they did not know what to call it, and they did it secretly. Boys were warned that the practice could drive them crazy, or blind, or both. They continued to do it—fearfully. Being an adolescent meant coping with values that colored all feelings of desire and curiosity with shame, guilt, and fear. It is not surprising that many married women could not enjoy sex; the prohibition against it was too strong to be dissolved by a wedding ceremony.

Those cruelly inhibiting values did have one advantage. They were

Photo by Michael Weisbrot

clear and unambiguous—as opposed to today's standards of behavior, which shift with the winds of a changeable society like sand on a windy beach. In the not-so-good-old days, for example, everyone knew that "nice" girls did not do "it." Many perfectly nice girls proceeded to do "it" all the same, but they knew they were breaking the rules. Those who were more experienced and knowledgeable had some information about protecting themselves; the more naive or unlucky ones became pregnant. This was the most frightening consequence imaginable, although less terrifying than in a previous generation, when suicide was often the only way out of this most shameful of circumstances.

Unfortunately, the double standard has not disappeared. As Lonnie Barbach noted in a recent conference, "Today's adolescents retain a 'bad girl-good girl' dichotomy, but now the classification depends not on whether or not the girl is a virgin but on whether or not she sleeps with her boyfriend or 'screws around.'"[1] Certainly the physical aspects of the teenage years have not changed. Adolescent boys continue to be embarrassed by erections. In the past, they sometimes tried to hide the evidence of their nocturnal emissions, just as Virgie had destroyed the evidence of her maturation. While today's adolescent male is usually not upset about wet dreams, unwanted erections still cause consternation.

In the late 1940s and 1950s, changes in society sparked changes in attitudes toward sexuality. The cooperative nursery school movement encouraged parents to be open, honest, and accepting with their children. Whereas masturbation once caused concern, the absence of it now raised questions. Was this youngster too timid, the parents too rigid? Was this teenager who seemed more interested in playing the piano than playing the field a neurotic, maladjusted youngster?

Alfred Kinsey's landmark *Sexual Behavior in the Human Male*, published in 1948, changed Americans' understanding of who actually did what in sexual matters. Ongoing social changes and shifting values culminated in the celebration of all things sexual that marked the 1960s and early 1970s—the period during which my own children experienced adolescence. Only in retrospect do I recognize how much of my own value system was shaped by those decades and how much I overtly and covertly passed on to my children, just as my mother did with me and as my children do with their children.

It was indeed an era of liberation—liberation from fear and shame. The pill promised that fear of pregnancy would never again inhibit the joy of sex. "Wonder drugs" promised to reverse the effects of venereal diseases. Society promised that the unmarried need not be surreptitious about their sexual activities or forced into an unsuitable marriage as the only respectable way to meet sexual needs. Even homosexuality gained in acceptability as a legitimate and normal variation of human sexuality.

Today, many of those who were teenagers in the era of "if it feels good, do it" have adolescent children of their own. In the intervening years, attitudes have undergone yet another shift. We learned that the pill was not a fully satisfactory answer to unplanned pregnancy. Some strains of gonorrhea proved resistant to antibiotics; herpes and other sexually transmitted diseases emerged as growing concerns (often irresponsibly exaggerated by the media); and AIDS threatened to become a global epidemic. We also became aware of the large number of individuals who were victims of childhood sexual abuse. For many, fear and sex are again linked.

Current Challenges

As a psychotherapist and a teacher of human sexuality, I face the challenges shared by all of us who want our young people to experience their sexuality in joyous and healthy ways. One of these challenges is dealing with the sensationalist crisis-mode response to problems prevalent in our society. This emphasis on "what can go wrong" obscures the deep, intense, enduring emotions that make sexuality so much more than "coupling."

When the Surgeon General of the United States recommended sex education in the schools, for example, it was for the express purpose of combating AIDS. Missing from officialdom is the recognition that education is needed to promote attitudes and behaviors that are emotionally as well as physiologically healthy. Missing, too, is the understanding that sexuality education does not begin or end in a classroom. It starts in infancy, with the related experience of sensuality. The enjoyment of one's sensual powers—one's ability to be keenly aware of and responsive to everything the senses receive—is an inherent part of human nature and is not dependent on sexual activity.

The fact that sexuality is related to self-esteem and self-worth presents another challenge. Youngsters who love themselves, who have a positive self-concept, are less likely to become involved in harmful activities. Adolescence is, by definition, a period of struggling to feel okay about oneself. Puberty brings a heightened awareness of every real or imagined physical deficiency. Even adolescents raised in a home environment of loving acceptance and regard are susceptible to viewing their bodies with dismay and to seeing themselves as unappealing, especially when compared with the impossibly gorgeous creatures portrayed in the media.

Adolescents need reassurance and reminders that in the real world, desirability and lovability do not depend on porcelain skin or "tight buns." They also need our recognition of the fact that appearance *does* sometimes count.

Unfortunately, those parents who want to encourage self-esteem in their teenagers find that their opinions are often dismissed. It is true that at this age, there is no validation as important as that from peers. Nonetheless, adolescents do want and need honest parental approval of many facets of their lives. Your reaction to a hairdo may not count, but your comments about abilities and talents, judgments and opinions, have more impact than you may think.

Comments such as these have a definite bearing on a teenager's sense of self-worth and thus his or her sexuality: "I'm not sure whether to use a plain or flowered upholstery for the sofa. You have such a good sense of color. What do you think?" "I'm impressed with how much you know about cars. It's a good thing you remind me to change the oil regularly!" "You really look terrific on the tennis court. I guess you have natural athletic ability."

Sexuality education rests on two main supports: information and attitude. Of these, attitude is the more important. Balancing information and attitude presents a third challenge. A positive, open attitude encourages the acquisition of information and makes it easily available; information in an emotional vacuum cannot be fully integrated.

One advantage of a school sexuality education program is the conveyed message that the topic is valid. School administrations recognize and support the need for adolescents to have information at their disposal and provide the personnel who are comfortable discussing it. However, the role of the parent in providing a healthy outlook is crucial. This does *not* mean that you must be a perfect parent with a totally wonderful family and no emotional hang-ups about sexuality. You need only be honest, aware, and available.

A fourth challenge is to be aware of the mixed messages being given to today's teenagers. Because of the fact that there may be a wide age span between present-day parents, teachers, other influential adults and teenagers, the social climate of your child's adolescence may be quite distant from your own. In addition, today's young people have received an unrealistic set of opposing values. The media and popular music bombard their senses with images of steamy sex, available sex, recreational sex, hot sex, fantastic sex, required sex; yet at the same time, we as parents have extolled delayed gratification, resistance to peer pressure, "mature" decision making. We need to be sensitive to this dilemma to deal with it effectively.

One interesting factor here is the changing sexual mores of older adults. Many adolescents see their divorced parents enjoying sexual relationships that are healthy, open, and stimulating. The interaction between long-married partners is not sexually charged in the way that dating, courtship, and "honeymoon" relations are. Even if this ardor on the part of divorced parents could be dampened, I for one would not recommend it; instead, simply recognize its influence on the youngsters in the family.

Although the very real difficulties faced by single-parent families are frequently chronicled, the advantages are rarely explored. One is that single parents frequently have more empathy with their adolescent children in the areas of dating, fear of rejection, and sexual urgency. Parents living in a long-established monogamous relationship may view these phenomena as transitory or trivial.

Another favorable look at single-parent families appears in the book *Being Adolescent*:

> When thousands of self-reports were averaged, it was found that children from one-parent families rated themselves overall as significantly more strong, free, clear, and skilled; and they tended to see their goals as more congruent with those of the people around them. . . . Apparently, living with only one adult simplifies a teenager's perception of what a situation requires. All of these dimensions of experience point to the single-parent child feeling more mature and autonomous. It is as if a single-parent family system provides a more favorable context for an adolescent who is already in the process of leaving that system.[2]

This is not to suggest that single parenting is a superior family style but rather to note that it can be a satisfactory one.

Reframing the Issues

The highly publicized hazards of sexually transmitted diseases— AIDS, herpes, chlamydia, gonorrhea, genital warts, and more—post a pronounced challenge to the development of adolescent sexuality. Parents and teachers can help to offset, or even avert, the damaging influence of sensational news reports by reframing the issues for teens.

One approach is to replace the term "safe sex" with "healthy sex." Explore the ramifications of this distinction and encourage your teenager to consider the many activities we participate in that are healthy but not necessarily safe. Reframing hysterical warnings into reasonable cautions is effective. Life has always been hazardous. We

Photo by Michael Weisbrot

can be so focused on the dangers that we deprive ourselves of joie de vivre; or we can deny the existence of the hazards and unnecessarily jeopardize ourselves; or we can do our best to take care of ourselves while enthusiastically living full, rich lives. Let your teenager know which approach you value the most.

In the excellent book *No Is Not Enough*, the authors address the question of sexual assault. They note that teens who understand that sex is used in a variety of ways are able to recognize potentially abusive situations and persons.[3]

Reframing the issues with your adolescent entails engaging in open dialogue and transmitting clear values that will endure the passage of time. Here are some important points to communicate:

1. Just as some people distort the natural need for food, some people indulge in sex when there is no real desire or use it to degrade another person.

2. The ability of partners to be responsible for their actions determines whether sex is "good" or "bad." Although different families have different standards, every value system requires responsibility. Some perceive the essential condition to be marriage; others consider it to be mutual caring. My personal bottom line is that there be no exploitation and that respect be shown for one's self and one's partner.

3. Equality between partners needs to be present for consent to be valid. Explain that relationships such as teacher/student or adult/teen are unequal and that consent in such situations may not be real.

4. Human sexual behavior is based on biological need but expressed in cultural terms. Talking about this can help explore and clarify some common uses ("good" and "bad") for sex, including reproduction, affection, expressing, power, creating bonds, being part of a crowd, rebelling, and release of tension.

These kinds of discussions keep the lines of communication open and lively and make a statement about your availability and willingness to do more than sermonize.

Communicating Effectively

Adults who are open about their own values are likely to be respected and respectful. Adults who acknowledge their own feelings make it easier for teenagers to be in touch with and expressive of their feelings.

Good communication requires accepting all feelings while setting realistic limits on behavior. When a three-year-old prepares to bash his baby brother, the enlightened parent differentiates feelings from behavior by preventing the bashing while acknowledging the rage. This parenting skill is invaluable in helping a teenager deal with the issues of sexuality.

Although effective communication does facilitate problem solving, it is neither a prevent-all nor a cure-all. In spite of everything, adolescents, like adults, make some poor judgments and have some bad luck. Unwanted teenage pregnancy, for instance, occurs even with adequate information and caring, available parents. When family communication has been honest and respectful, chances are much greater that the adolescent will quickly turn to the family for help and guidance and will arrive at the best decision regarding a course of action. If the family's response is punitive, cold, unavailable, or arbitrary, the problem of pregnancy is compounded, and the stage is set for future difficulties.

Effective communication depends primarily on three attributes:

Honesty. Say what you mean and mean what you say. If your youngster attends a party that you understood would be chaperoned, and you learn that the parents were actually out of town, your response can make a difference. You can be dishonest and lay a trap by asking, "Did you have a chance to talk to Val's parents last night? How are they?" Or you can be honest and say, "I heard that Val's parents have been out of town and the party last night was unchaperoned. I'm upset about this and want to talk to you." Dealing directly with the problem at hand models honesty in communication.

Respect. Be sensitive to issues of privacy, knowledge, and self-esteem. An example: "I'm not sure just how much you know about birth control and disease protection. Sometimes it's hard for us to talk about this kind of thing, but I really need to be sure that you have the necessary information, so let's stumble through this."

Listening. This is a twofold process. It means remaining attentive while the other party speaks and making an honest, respectful effort to understand opinions, excitements, and fears.

Many useful books are available to help develop effective communication skills. *Between Parent and Teenager* by the late Haim Ginott is especially valuable. Remember, though, that all professional advice, including what appears here, should be taken with a generous helping of "Easy to say, but it never works quite that way!"

In both family and group settings, communication is enhanced when both genders participate and when controversial or potentially frightening subjects are addressed with sensitivity. The following observations are distilled from experiences in school programs. However, the points they illustrate apply to family situations as well.

For reasons that are not quite clear, adolescent boys generally tend to be much more reserved than girls in open discussions about sexuality. This in itself is a compelling reason to consider coeducational involvement and, if possible, male and female instructors. Coeducational discussions and role-playing sessions are informative, sometimes astonishing, and always helpful in conveying additional points of view. They also allow teenagers to learn to understand and communicate with each other *now*, in the dating years, before long-term commitments are made.

In addition, coeducational participation yields insights into experiences that may not be addressed elsewhere in the teen's immediate world. The role of the adolescent father in unwanted pregnancy is taken on in some school programs by having boys and girls participate in a nonverbal exercise. They are instructed to carry a five-pound bag of sugar with them wherever they go, keep the bag warmly wrapped, "feed" it every few hours, and above all, never leave it alone. Having boys as well as girls participate demonstrates the responsibility of impregnating as well as becoming pregnant.

When I began teaching sexuality education courses about eight years ago, the most controversial area was homosexuality. I indicated to parents and teachers that I believed this topic should be discussed along with the other dimensions of sexuality, and I was often met with disbelief, acute discomfort, and sometimes strong disapproval. Many parents and educators who supported informed discussion on birth control and sexually transmitted diseases drew the line at homosexuality. In these instances, I compromised by making the following statement to the students: "Some of you may have feelings and fantasies that you think are abnormal. Maybe you think *you* are abnormal. There is one thing I can tell you absolutely and positively. Everything you feel or think about is shared by some other people. It's important that you have someplace to discuss these things. If you like, I'll make a private appointment to chat with you."

Now most parents *want* me to discuss homosexuality, although frequently they hope I will present a fearful picture. Instead, I discuss the extreme pain, guilt, and isolation often experienced by adolescents having homosexual desires. I tell them about support groups such as Parents and Friends of Lesbians and Gays.[4] I share my own belief system, which is basically that homosexuality and heterosexuality form a continuum, and that we still have much to learn about why different individuals are in different places along the continuum. In addition, I remain personally available for consultation.

The implications for sexuality development are challenging. The important point is to keep lines of communication open. If you and your teen wish to delve into some reading on the topic, be sure to include plenty of fiction. *The Last Picture Show*, by Larry McMurtry, is a story of male adolescence from a perspective that may be disturbing but is also enlightening. *The Summer of My German Soldier*, by Bette Greene, portrays the romantic, idealized love that eases a young girl's desperate loneliness. *In a Different Voice*, a nonfiction book by Carol Gilligan, explores the formation of values.

As in all things adolescent, sexuality is characterized by mercurial changes, intense feelings, confusion, developmental dangers and delights, paradoxes, pain, pleasure, and growth. Mary Calderone and James Ramey, in their book *Talking with Your Child about Sex*, capture the essence charmingly by quoting from R. D. Laing's *Knots*:

> There is something I don't know
>   that I am supposed to know.
> I don't know what it is I don't know,
>   and yet am supposed to know,
> and I feel I look stupid
>   if I seem both not to know it
>   and not to know what it is I don't know.
> Therefore I pretend I know it.
>   this is nerve-racking
>   since I don't know what I must pretend
>   to know.
> Therefore I pretend to know everything.
>
> I feel you know what I am supposed to know
> but you can't tell me what it is
> because you don't know that I don't know
>   what it is.
> You may know what I don't know, but not
>   that I don't know it,
> and I can't tell you. So you will have to tell me
>   everything.[5]

Notes

1. Barbach, Lonnie, "Relationships and the New Sexual Climate," a talk presented at the Gestalt Therapy Institute of Los Angeles (January 23, 1988).

2. Csikszentmihalyi, Mihaly, and Reed Larson, *Being Adolescent* (New York: Basic Books, 1984).

3. Adams, Caren, et al., *No Is Not Enough* (San Luis Obispo, Calif.: Impact Publishers, 1987), chap. 9.

4. Federation of Parents and Friends of Lesbians and Gays, P.O. Box 24565, Los Angeles, CA 90024.

5. Calderone, Mary, and James W. Ramey, *Talking with Your Child about Sex* (New York: Random House, 1986), frontispiece.

Bibliography

Adams, Caren, et al. *No Is Not Enough*. San Luis Obispo, Calif.: Impact Publishers, 1987.

Calderone, Mary, and James W. Ramey. *Talking with Your Child about Sex*. New York: Random House, 1986.

Csikszentmihalyi, Mihaly, and Reed Larson. *Being Adolescent*. New York: Basic Books, 1984.

Editorial. "Boys: The Forgotten Partners," *The Hartford Courant*, October 31, 1987.

Ginott, Haim. *Between Parent and Teenager*. New York: Avon, 1971.

Greene, Bette. *Summer of My German Soldier*. Toronto: Bantam Books, 1973.

Lerner, Richard M., and Nancy L. Galambos, eds. *Experiencing Adolescence: A Sourcebook for Parents, Teachers, and Teens*. New York: Garland Publishing, 1984.

McMurtry, Larry. *The Last Picture Show*. New York: Dial Press, 1966.

Madaras, Lynda. *Growing Up Guide for Girls* (New York: Newmarket, 1986).

——. *What's Happening to My Body? Book for Boys* (New York: Newmarket, 1987).

——. *What's Happening to My Body? Book for Girls* (New York: Newmarket, 1987).

8

PUBERTY'S CHILD

Candy Schock

Your hormonal anger
pins me to the ceiling
with darts soaked in
Super Glue.

I could go—
would go—
and wing my way away.

But the stuff of
Love demands
steadfastness.
I'm very
good
at

sticking.

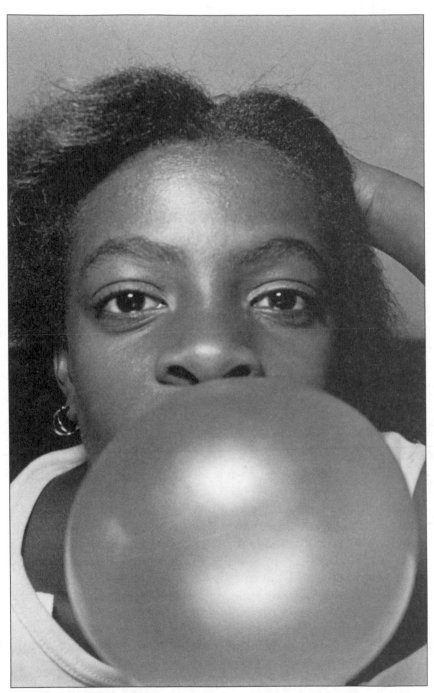

Photo by Michael Weisbrot

9

TEENAGE PREGNANCY

Lorraine Vissering

Teen pregnancy. The words are likely to conjure up images of children having children; youngsters who are not quite ready or able to assume the awesome responsibility of nurturing a new life but who go ahead and do so anyway. Perhaps the words *accident* or *irresponsible* come to mind. Maybe feelings of frustration surface, along with a wish that something could be done to stop the "epidemic," to prevent this current generation of children from producing yet more kids destined for poverty, lack of education, broken homes, and broken dreams.

We need to replace such fearful images with realistic insights based on fact. Key questions need to be answered. What *is* it like to be very young and pregnant? What *are* the needs and wants of young pregnant women? How can we as adults offer *truly* supportive guidelines?

My Story

I became pregnant at fifteen, as a direct result of unprotected sex, and as an indirect result of a it-won't-happen-to-*me* attitude. I had briefly entertained the idea of birth control pills but quickly realized I did not know the first thing about how to go about obtaining them. I had never been to a gynecologist, had no money, and had never heard of family planning clinics. Nor did I have access to an understanding adult who could help me. In addition, none of my friends who were sexually active used birth control.

So, after approximately nine months of fairly regular, completely unprotected sex, I became pregnant. At this time, I had only just begun to menstruate and had had only three periods at irregular intervals. Three or four months after my third period, I began to feel tired and nauseated. My mother noticed my "sickness" and took me to the local ob-gyn practice. The first doctor I saw was brusque,

Photo by Michael Weisbrot

fast, and silent as he examined me. He did not tell me what to expect or what the procedure would entail, and I was too afraid and nervous to ask. When the nurse took my medical history, I stared at the floor and answered nearly all her questions with "I don't know." I wondered if she had any idea how confused and frightened I was. I thought I might cry if I tried to tell her, and I did *not* want to look like a crybaby.

When the examination was over, my mother and I sat opposite the white-coated doctor behind his desk. (The scene was uncomfortably reminiscent of the time, one year earlier, when my mother and I had sat opposite the junior high school principal behind *his* desk and discussed my truancy.) I felt as though I had done something terribly wrong but was not completely sure what it was. The doctor looked at my mother and said perfunctorily, "She's pregnant. Everything seems to be okay right now, though I won't know for sure just *how* pregnant she is until we do an ultrasound." Then he stood up and asked my mother, "Any questions?" She queried him about vitamins and was handed a prescription. As she and I left the office, I wondered, what is ultrasound?

I was very much alone during my pregnancy. The father of my baby refused to acknowledge that he had anything to do with the situation and suddenly refused to have anything more to do with *me*. I soon decided that it was best this way. I was angry and hurt, but I came to the conclusion that a person who does not want to have a baby is better off not being forced to and that a baby should not have to live with a parent who does not want to be one.

I knew that *I* wanted my baby very much. The subject of adoption never came up. Likewise, the option of abortion was never presented. I knew vaguely what it was but could also imagine how it was done; and after my harrowing experience at the doctor's office, I wasn't about to visit any more health professionals voluntarily. I suppose it was a commonly, if silently, agreed-upon fact that I would both have and keep my baby. If I wanted assistance, my family would help me care for the baby.

At that time my family consisted of my mother (a single parent herself), my two older sisters, myself, and my two younger brothers. My mother had never completed high school and had no job training or skills that could help her support a family of six. As a result, we lived on welfare payments. I knew I did not want to raise my child on the subsistence income that welfare affords. I also knew that I had no

other choice as long as I was still in school. My family was in no position to assist me financially, but my mother and sisters let me know
that they would help me by accepting my child as a member of the
family and by providing free child care when they could so that I
could finish school. Two women with whom our family was friendly
had had children when they were teenagers, and both had been pressured to put their babies up for adoption—a decision they both later
regretted. I was lucky. Knowing that my family was there to support
and help me with my baby made it easier for me to have and keep my
child.

But no one mentioned the physical changes, sensations, feelings, or
experiences that might come my way during the pregnancy and birth.
I knew from watching television that women having babies are prone
to pant, gasp, get sweaty, and maybe even scream once or twice. I
also suspected that the doctors would have a variety of shots, pills,
and gas they could administer if the pain became too great. For the
most part, I simply tried not to think about the birth.

I tried, but I did not always succeed. I lay awake many nights block-
ing out thoughts about what it might be like to give birth. My greatest
solace was a fervent, consuming wish to have a baby girl who would
look just like me. I imagined what she would look like as a one-year-
old and as a five-year-old. I imagined how I would dress her, take her
for walks, and play with her; how I would raise her and love her; and
how she would always be happy and protected and provided for.
These musings held my fears at bay for short periods of time. More
often, though, my mind was crowded with nightmares of pain, mal-
formed babies, and incompetence. How would I *really* provide for my
child? Having spent my childhood on welfare, I did not want my child
to do the same. In short, I was terrified.

With each visit to the doctor's office, I grew more anxious and confused. Lying there naked, I was poked, prodded, questioned, and then
left alone. Neither the receptionists, nurses, nor doctors—it seemed as
though I never saw the same person twice—were particularly open or
warm, nor did they share information with me or ask if I had any
questions. No one suggested a book that might help me understand
the physical changes that were occurring. No one suggested a person
who might be able to just talk things over with me. I did not know
any other pregnant people, of any age.

It is true that, had someone approached me with help of any kind, I would probably have been wary. I was already suspicious of social workers; I clearly remembered the welfare lady who had come to our house and asked my mother, "Well, have you even *tried* looking for a job?" She did not ask if we had gotten the heat turned back on yet or if we needed diapers or food; she asked if we owned real estate, stocks, or bonds. Perhaps if someone had made it clear that he or she was there not to judge me but to help me figure out how to get help or information, I might have been receptive. Either way, the opportunity did not arise.

The doctor said I was due in late April. During the first two weeks of March, I began feeling exceptionally uncomfortable and was unable to sleep. One night I sat on the toilet until daybreak, trying to pee and feeling very short of breath. Just before dawn, when I noticed a small amount of bloody mucus floating in the toilet, I was sure I was losing the baby. My mother and I went to the doctor's office for what turned out to be my final prenatal examination.

This visit was the worst one yet. All I wanted to do was crouch on my knees and curl up into a ball, not lie flat on my back and spread my legs. Again, my mother and I concluded the visit by sitting across the desk from the doctor. This time, he looked right at my mother and said, "She *is* in labor. I'll meet her over at the hospital. We'll do a cesarean. It should take about an hour." Walking out of the office, I wondered, what is a cesarean? Only when my mother surrendered me to a wheelchair and I heard the word *admissions* did everything sink in. So this is *it*, I thought, and I closed my eyes.

The next hour or so was the most humiliating, agonizing, and frightening time of my life. The machines were cold; faceless, white-clothed, fast-moving people spoke to each other in a language I did not understand. They did bizarre things to me: a "prep" I was not prepared for, a wrapping of Ace bandages too tightly around my legs, and an application of orange liquid that coated my belly. During it all, only one person spoke directly to *me*. This was a young nurse with a clipboard, who asked me if I was planning to keep my baby.

I was bewildered, angry, and in pain. Finally, I was turned onto my side and felt a needle crunching through the cartilage between two vertebrae. Then I felt a slow, numbing warmth consume my entire body from the neck on down. I wondered if I would ever feel anything again.

Thankfully, I did. I survived, and three days later I was sufficiently

Photo by Michael Weisbrot

recovered from the effects of the medication to meet my daughter. I did not nurse Carrie because I had no idea how to, and no one offered to help me. My interest in breast-feeding was further complicated by pain from the surgery, a "spinal headache," high dosages of pain medication, and engorged breasts. With no support for or knowledge about how to begin breast-feeding, I accepted the nurses' offer to bind my breasts with Ace bandages and give me a shot to "dry up my milk."

After a week-long hospital stay, my daughter and I went home. I could not lift Carrie, or even stand straight, for an entire month. But I could hold her and look at her. I felt oddly removed, distant, and separated from her. But I was completely awed by her. I still am, nine and a half years later.

Toward a New Awareness

The discussions I have had over the past nine years with other pregnant and parenting teens have convinced me that my experience is not unique. Many young women go through a pregnancy and birth intimidated by their own ignorance and receiving no help, support, or education from those in a position to offer it.

Teenage women who are pregnant, especially those who have learned not to question authority, are particularly susceptible to the treatment they receive from busy professionals. Often those women are isolated, ignored, or simply left alone. Sometimes they are inundated with contradictory advice and placed under extreme pressure to do the "right" thing, which can change with each person they talk to. Sometimes they are more fortunate and receive the information they want and need on many aspects of pregnancy, childbirth, parenting, and family planning. And sometimes they are doubly fortunate and are given the emotional and moral support that enables them to make truly informed decisions, decisions that *they* know are right for both themselves and their children-to-be. Decisions of this magnitude should not be made passively; they should not be decided by not deciding.

Teenage women who are pregnant are also uniquely vulnerable to developmental and social influences. Most teenagers are likely to go through periods of self-doubt and insecurity, especially when choosing life goals; but pregnant teenagers are more obviously caught between childhood and adulthood. Being pregnant and making decisions about parenting are distinctly "grown-up" things to do. However, a young woman of fourteen, fifteen, or sixteen years of age tends not to be regarded as an adult by the parents, teachers, health care practitioners, and other influential figures in her world. Sensitivity to both her developmental needs and her personal need to be involved in decision making is critical. Significant adults in her world must let her *know* that she can ask for help. In my case, I believe I would have found it helpful if a friendly but *not* condescending adult had given me some basic information on pregnancy, childbirth, and caring for an infant. I did go to *one* of the hospital-sponsored childbirth classes, but I never went back, because I didn't want to be the only single person of my age in a room full of people who looked like my parents, my teachers, and my doctors.

Some people argue that teenagers should not have sex to begin with. Not all teens do; but it is estimated that by age eighteen, only 20 percent of boys and 30 percent of girls are still virgins. More than 1.1 million pregnancies occur among teenagers every year in the United States. Forty-nine percent of pregnant teens decide to have their babies, and 93 percent of those who do, decide to keep them.[1] Regardless of whether it is right or wrong, it is clear that teens are having sex, and it seems realistic to assume that they will continue to do so.

It is important to realize that all teenage pregnancies are *not* tragedies. Every teenage mother is not a sad statistic signifying a wasted life and potential for child abuse. When truly interested, respectful, and caring people reach out in nonpressuring, nonjudgmental, and creative ways to offer support and education to teens, the chances are very good that they will respond by accepting the offer. Teenagers *do* have the right to make informed decisions. They *do* deserve respect and support in their decision making.

Finally, as inadequate as the welfare system may be, it does *not* have to be the end of the road. A teenager who makes the decision to be a parent deserves all the help and support she can get. Whether she is on welfare or getting off it, caring people can provide her with the kind of help she needs to make it. Given today's statistics, it is clear that pregnant teenagers are a reality. In order to give them and their babies the best possible chance in life, we need to treat them as individuals with special needs rather than faceless facets of a larger "problem."

Notes

1. Adolescent pregnancy data compiled by the Adolescent Pregnancy Prevention Task Force, Planned Parenthood Federation of America, 1984.

For More Information

Ashford, Janet Isaacs, ed. *Birth Stories.* Freedom, Calif.: The Crossing Press, 1984.

Barr, Linda, and Catherine Monserrat. *Teenage Pregnancy: A New Beginning.* Albuquerque, N.M.: New Futures Inc., 1978.

Bell, Ruth, and Leni Zeiger Wildflower. *Talking with Your Teenager: A Book for Parents.* New York: Random House, 1983.

Bell, Ruth, and others. *Changing Bodies, Changing Lives: A Book for Teens on Sex and Relationships.* New York: Random House, 1980.

Bingham, Mindy, Judy Edmondsom, and Sandy Stryker. *Choices: A Teen Woman's Journal for Self-Awareness and Personal Discovery.* Santa Barbara: Advocacy Press, 1987.

Brazelton, T. Berry. *Infants and Mothers—Differences in Development.* New York: Dell Publishing Co., 1985.

Eisenberg, Arlene, et al. *What to Expect When You Are Expecting.* New York: Workman Publishing, 1984.

Evans, Judith, and Ellen Ilfeld. *Good Beginnings—Parenting in the Early Years.* Ypsilanti, Mich.: High Scope Press, 1982.

Lindsay, Jeanne Warren. *Open Adoption: A Caring Option.* Buena Park, Calif.: Morning Glory Press, 1987.

Kitzinger, Sheila. *Your Baby, Your Way: Making Pregnancy Decisions and Birth Plans.* New York: Pantheon Books, 1987.

PARENTS AND TEENS

Don Dinkmeyer

Communication is the building block of any effective relationship. It breathes energy into the relationship and enables those involved to work toward common goals. We often fail to understand that communication is a two-way process—talking and listening. The major problem in parent-teen relationships is that it appears no one is listening. Unless there is listening, there is no communication. Very often when we observe a parent-teen relationship, we will hear the complaint: "They just don't understand me. They don't care. They never listen. I don't feel I'm being heard." This is heard as often from teens as it is heard from parents.

Many households have lots of "communication" going on: "Stop that." "I'm going to do it anyhow." "You aren't respecting me." "You won't do that as long as you live here." However, it is only when the other person hears, comprehends, accepts, and is willing to negotiate in terms of our beliefs, values, and standards that real communication starts. Commands, demands, and complaints usually stimulate a retort but almost never facilitate any true mutual understanding.

Communication is a process that works best between equals who are concerned and care about each other. Communication, thus, is not on a vertical but on a horizontal or level plane. Vertical communication attempts to insist, demand, or boss, and thus creates distance between those involved. An example: "You will be in when I say so. You'll do it my way or not at all." This type of communication very often results in "parent deafness" on the part of the teens. They simply refuse to listen.

The first step you as a parent should take in communicating with your child is to develop an open, honest, congruent relationship in which you can express your feelings directly, and your teen can also.

Photo by Michael Weisbrot

Make no demands; require only that you each listen, understand, and attempt to negotiate a more effective relationship. In this type of communication, you seek cooperation and mutual goals. Things do not have to go only your way. When your child perceives this caring on your part, cooperation is usually increased.

Much family conversation is "business conversation." This deals primarily with the everyday affairs of the family and is often a series of commandments, "demandments," requests, and suggestions, with little sharing of feelings and beliefs. As a result, teens often feel that they are in the company of people who are serving as "commanders-in-chief"; people who operate as judges, evaluating and pronouncing judgment on their feelings; people who serve primarily as critics. These perceptions tend to interrupt and interfere with the development of effective parent-teen communication.

As a parent, ask yourself some simple questions:

Can I be honest with my teenager? Do I really say what I feel and what I believe, sharing it in a nonhurtful way? Test this in terms of topics like school, boy/girl relations, friendships, and cooperation in household chores.

Can my teen be open and honest with me? If he or she shares what he or she believes, feels, and values, and it is different from what I expect, am I still able to accept and understand these beliefs and feelings? Do I listen before debating or retorting? If I were a teen, would I come to me to reveal a feeling or a goal?

Do I have the courage to be honest and give feedback? Feedback does not demand change but only states how one person is experiencing another. It then leaves the decision about change with the person who is receiving feedback.

Am I willing and open to receiving feedback from my teenager? Unless you are courageous enough to share your feelings and perceptions and open the door for your teens to share their beliefs and perceptions with you, it is very difficult to start an effective communication process.

One of the problems involved in the communication process with teens is the issue of "problem ownership." If you as a parent feel you need to be involved in every aspect of your teen's life, if all problems your teen has are your problems, then communication will be perpetually ineffective. When you insist on taking charge of your teen's problems, you are encouraging dependence or perhaps rebellion. Most important, you are denying the teen the opportunity to develop responsibility in the handling of his or her problems.

It is essential that parents let teens handle their own problems. This is the only way they will mature and become effective adults. As a parent, you can be available to listen, understand, and provide guidance as requested, but when the problem belongs to the teen, avoid "owning" the problem.

Now you may be asking, "How do you decide who owns the problem?" The following simple questions can help clarify this issue.

Does this problem interfere with my rights and responsibilities?

Does it involve the safety of my teen or others?

If the answer is no to either of these questions, it is not your problem. Also ask yourself: who is experiencing the problem, and with whom? Your teen may be in conflict with a teacher, your spouse, a friend, or a sibling. But the problem is between the teen and another person. At that point your most effective course of action is to let the teen take care of the problem on his or her own.

It is important that you also acknowledge and take responsibility for your own feelings. One will often hear a parent saying about a teen, "He makes me so angry," or "What's happening to her makes me so sad." In such a situation, own your feelings. They are not *caused* by the teen. *Feelings are under your control.* You have the capacity to choose a different type of feeling. It is important to be aware of how we sometimes use feelings to achieve our own purposes. If we feel hurt, perhaps we are hoping others will feel sorry for us. If we feel angry, maybe others will give in and thus end the power struggle.

An effective communicator in a parent-teen relationship is one who is able to get into a reflective listening mode. You can always learn more when you are listening than when you are talking. Don't interrupt, but stop, look, and listen.

Reflective listening is a way to show that the message has been understood. You become a mirror that helps teens see themselves and their own feelings more clearly. For example, your daughter comes home and says, "I tried out for the chorus and I didn't make it because there were just too many good singers." You might say, "You feel discouraged because you didn't make the chorus." When you reflectively listen, you do not merely repeat what your teen says. Instead, you restate your teen's message, picking up the feelings and adding words to what he or she is trying to say.

When people express their feelings, they usually don't use feeling words. One reason for this is that most of us have been discouraged from expressing any negative feelings. Another reason is that when we are upset, we often don't think as clearly. But it is important to learn how to listen closely for unarticulated feelings in conversation and to phrase reflective listening responses. It is also important to have teenagers share their feelings so they can handle the many turbulent emotions that they are experiencing.

In order to become an effective communicator in this way, you need to listen closely to what your teen is saying. As you begin reflective listening, you may feel most comfortable by using a simple format, such as "you feel . . . because. . . ." This formula can and should be varied in the natural flow of the conversation. It is also important to be aware of the difference between an open and a closed response. Open responses show that you understand what your teen is attempting to communicate. Closed responses imply you haven't really understood what your teen has said. The closed response often passes judgment, interprets, and analyzes. It tells the teen how to feel, it gives advice, and it often fails to respect the teen's feelings. Closed responses are usually interpreted by teens as blaming responses that take away their responsibility. An open response understands their feelings and the circumstances associated with these feelings.

Here are some simple guidelines to effective communication skills:

Be aware of your true feelings and thoughts and share your awareness. This involves getting in touch with yourself and being sensitive to what you are experiencing. It also involves sharing openly and honestly what you have experienced. Obviously your model of this and all other communication skills will show your teen a more effective way of relating. Your awareness assures you are not holding back your feelings and beliefs for a later day. Nor are you masking or pretending what you feel. The communication process thus begins by being tuned in to your own feelings and by being willing to share them courageously.

When you share feelings, do so in an open, caring way. Listen to your teen empathetically and patiently. Communication clearly is a two-way connection. When you share your feelings, do it with an "I" message that does not communicate blame to the listener. When our teens don't listen, it is often because we send them "you" messages instead of "I" messages. "You" messages are statements that tend to put teens down. They blame and criticize. Very often they provoke anger, hurt, embarrassment, and a feeling of worthlessness. The "I" message is an alternative to the "you" message. For example, instead of saying, "You make me very angry," say "I'm feeling very angry." An "I" message simply shares our feelings and concerns and communicates that we trust our teens to respect our feelings. When we use "I" messages, we never imply that teens "make us feel angry or hurt," but we assert that we are responsible for our own emotions, that we are in charge of our feelings.

Share meanings to be sure you understand each other. It has been observed and demonstrated on countless occasions that while we may think we understand what our teen means, we often do not. Thus, there must be a continual clarification and sharing of what the teen's message meant to us. You can do this by asking questions and double-

Photo by Hildegard Adler

checking answers. "What I was experiencing was . . . ." "Were you say-ing . . . ?" "It seems to me . . . ." "You believe . . . ." Take time to hear and explore. If you find that you are not correct, ask her or him to tell you more about it.

Share intentions. Teens are often unclear about what it is that parents want. It may seem to them that their parents want total control, power, and the ability to make all kinds of decisions, to essentially "own" their life. Let your teen know what you want for yourself in your relationship. It is important for you to establish mutually accept-able goals with your teen. It is equally important for you to identify what goals, intentions, ambitions, and priorities you have that may be keeping the relationship from being a more effective one.

Express ways in which you accept and value each other. Often much negative communication exists between the parent and teen, which makes it essential to understand and share positive feelings. Here it is important to understand the total encouragement process. Encouragement is the process of giving heart to the person whom you are communicating with. It affirms what is positive. It communicates your love and acceptance. It shares what you like and enjoy about the relationship. Through your enthusiasm, you actually can breathe energy into the relationship.

Give positive feedback. State what you are experiencing without making a demand for change. This feedback principle is essential in any relationship. Our feedback shares with teens how we experience them. It does not make a demand for change. Observe closely anything positive that is occurring in the relationship and comment on it.

Communicate negative thoughts and feelings in a caring manner. State your feelings sensitively so they are not perceived as an attack.

The major roadblock to better communication is our own egos. When we feel and insist we are right, there is no opportunity for listening to occur or dialogue to begin. However, when we develop mutual respect and an open, caring attitude that recognizes we, too, are imperfect, then we encourage communication to begin. As communication improves, problems in discipline, motivation, and cooperation are reduced.

The solution to a poor parent-teen relationship and ineffective communication lies with you, the parent. If you can approach the challenge with a sense of humor, you will find the barriers beginning to fall. To have a family life that is harmonious and fosters communication you need to focus on building your own and your teen's self-esteem, desire to cooperate, and sense of humor.

Bibliography

Carlson, Jon. "The Basics of Discipline." Coral Springs, Fla.: CMTI Press, Inc.

Dinkmeyer, Don. "Basics of Adult-Teen Relationships." Coral Springs, Fla.: CMTI Press, Inc.

Dinkmeyer, Don, Jr., and Jim Dinkmeyer. "The Basics of Parenting." Coral Springs. Fla.: CMTI Press, Inc.

Dinkmeyer, Don, and Lew Losoncy. *The Encouragement Book: Becoming a Positive Person.* New York: Prentice-Hall, 1991.

Dinkmeyer, Don, and Gary D. McKay. *Systematic Training for Effective Parenting (STEP).* Circle Pines, MN 55014. American Guidance Service, 1976. *STEP Handbook,* Random House, 1982.

——. *Systematic Training for Effective Parenting of Teens (STEP/TEEN).* American Guidance Service, 1983.

11

ADOLESCENCE

Tovaa Steckull

Don't tell me to
or not
cause then I won't
or will
you see.
It seems like the whole thing
is a tricky business
of how to be part of
and yet know myself to be
me alone
special
unique
one of a kind.

See?
That's all there is to it.

And you thought I had the flu.

Photo by John Schoenwalter Photography

COMMUNICATING WITH YOUR ADOLESCENT

Elizabeth Hormann

It was a scene out of every mother's wish book. My daughters were sprawled across my bed telling me about their day—and their evening—and yesterday—and the week before last. When one ran out of steam, the next picked up the conversation. Periodically the narrative was punctuated with, "So what do you think, Mom?" but they never waited for an answer. The talk flowed on, then slowed to a trickle. "I think we kept her up past her bedtime," one daughter said. I opened one eye. It was 2:00 a.m. When I had thought about communicating with my teenagers, I had had an earlier hour in mind! Still, we *were* communicating, and if the late hour prevented me from giving full attention (Okay, I did fall asleep, but only toward the end), I was trying to listen. My girls are very understanding about lapses of that sort. ("After all, she is over 40.")

Communication is one of the biggest issues between parents and teenagers. "She's so secretive," parents complain. "They never listen to me," counters the adolescent. Both want to communicate; each blames the other for the failure to do so. In most cases this failure does not result from a lack of goodwill but rather from a misunderstanding about what teenagers need to get from their relationship with their parents. It may also stem from a gradual drifting away from once-successful communication methods that could still prove useful as children grow older and develop their own lives.

What is it that teenagers want from their interactions with their parents? Nothing very complicated, as it turns out. They want to know that:

- You love them.
- You respect them. Growing up is all right.
- You trust them. You have faith that your upbringing will "take."

Photo by Michael Weisbrot

• You will stand by them. When they make their inevitable mistakes, you won't throw them to the wolves. They may have to bail themselves out, but they can count on you to help.

• You are interested in what they are doing and thinking. And (this may come as a surprise) they want to know what you are doing and thinking as well.

Letting you know what they need may not be the easiest thing in the world for your teens. In a society that prizes independence above all, adolescents have a hard time figuring out just how independent they have to be to be grown up. While they are working on this problem, they may adopt an "I-don't-need-you" stance, but they *do* need you, and they hope you know it even if they don't.

Communicating with your adolescent really begins in childhood; in the early days, with your responsiveness to his cries, your touch, the sound of your voice, the way you look your child in the eye. A paradox of parenthood is that parents tend to be the most eager and most creative in their efforts to communicate when communication is the most difficult, when they have to guess at the meaning of their child's every action. Is that a hungry cry or a tired cry? Is the baby sick or just lonely? In the first year of life parents hold and stimulate their children, talk and sing to them, literally coax language from them. Then, all too often, they stop. Once the child is verbal, they may assume he or she thinks very much like they do. He doesn't. Maturity lags well behind language development, and parents may become frustrated by the contrast between their child's verbal facility and his capacity for rational thought.

This contrast becomes very pronounced in adolescence. What parent of a teenager hasn't torn her hair and cried, "When are you *ever* going to grow up?" We need to make allowances for immaturity all along the way, gradually raising our expectations but also remembering just how long it took *us* to grow up.

It is helpful in communicating with adolescents if you have established some patterns earlier in life that carry over. Our earliest communications with our children are through touch. There is no arbitrary time when that should cease. Sometimes a hug or an arm around the shoulder or a back rub is the best way to communicate your concern and your love.

Thanks to a European husband, I was introduced to the family bed concept before it reappeared in this country. From infancy, the chil-

dren slept in my bed—full-time at first, then off and on as they gradually moved into beds of their own. Countless times of joy and sadness,
of quiet talk and rowdy tickling, and of silence that says more than
words have been shared because the children are free to wander into
my bed. This practice also acts as an early warning system when
something is wrong. If I come home from an evening out and find a
child or two in my bed, I am alerted to a problem. Night wandering,
no longer a routine, is a signal that the wanderer is bothered by something or maybe getting sick. The intimacy carries over during the day.
Hugs are daily fare. I can count on at least three out of a possible four
kisses before the children leave for school, and double occupancy is
the rule for chairs and sofas. The teenager who would die before saying, "I love you" (except to another teenager of opposite gender) asks
to be tucked in almost every night. I am happy to oblige.

Communication comes in other forms as well. I remember that
when I was in college, one of my favorite families gathered every day
to read aloud. Very often the father did the reading, but the mother
and children took turns as well. They went through a great many
good books in the course of each year. This practice laid a good
intellectual foundation for the children, but, more important, it was a
cherished ritual, a time of regular family contact, and a basis for much
pleasurable and heated discussion. As the children grew, the reading
became less regular, but whenever most of them were together, they
made a point to read aloud. This family was not without problems,
but early in their family life they established rituals that bound them
together and gave them happy memories and plenty to talk about.
Even today, the parents aging, the children all over forty, they talk
more when they get together than any family I know.

My family reads together, too, not quite so regularly, but often. Last
summer and fall, we went through the _Chronicles of Narnia_. We discussed the books and a dozen subjects they suggested for months
afterward. If we hadn't had this to talk about, we would have found
something else, because much of our family activity is structured to
encourage, but not force, talk. Take cooking, for example, which is
usually a multiperson activity. We can talk about recipes and food as
we stir and knead and slice and chop—and sometimes we do—but
very often something else comes up. A child may use this time to
bring up a problem or issue that has been on his mind, or the family
may get involved in a discussion. If the conversation lags, or we come

too close to a sore point, we can turn back to the task at hand without hurting feelings or embarrassing anyone. The subject can always be taken up again, perhaps at a later date.

We also talk while we are playing games and putting together puzzles. This is a way to be together without feeling pressured to communicate. In such situations my kids can explore a subject as far as they want—and no further. Playing games with my children also gives me great insight into their personalities and moods. Are they deeply engrossed or distracted? Bent on winning or more relaxed? How do they respond to frustration? To being on top?

Talking in the midst of a shared project is companionable but also more than that. The project creates an atmosphere that is not threatening. No one *has* to talk; yet because there is no pressure, people are more likely to open up. There is something to occupy hands and minds as thoughts are aired and tested. Just sharing in a project is good nonverbal communication. By building a bookshelf, paddling a canoe, or baking bread, parents and children are developing skills together. Often they take joint pride in what they have created, and new bonds are forged between them.

I don't mean to imply that we never just talk. We do. We sit down and talk over the bread or cookies we have baked; we talk when the children come home from school; we talk by appointment—at my request or theirs; and we talk a lot about the business of family living. This is probably the area that is most fraught with difficulty. "Where are you going?" "Who are you going to be with?" "When are you going to: clean your room, do your homework, pick up the piles of clothing in the bathroom?"

Adolescents are in the business of testing limits. They want to take control over their lives. This is indeed something they should begin to do, or they won't know how when they are really grown up. But they still need parents to give them some guidelines and boundaries. Each family has to work out what guidelines are suitable for them. For order and peace of mind, most families insist on knowing where their children are, whom they are with, and when they are coming back. And most teenagers ask, "Don't you trust me?" at some time. Trust isn't the issue here, but courtesy and security. People in families need to know how to reach each other. When one of them is away, it is helpful to know approximately when that person will return. This rule applies as much to parents as it does to their children. My chil-

Photo by Hildegard Adler

dren have griped about this, but gradually they have come to realize that asking these questions is not a reflection on them or on their friends but simply good sense. One evening recently my college-age daughter, home for a visit, came flying down the stairs just as I was about to go out, demanding, "Where are you going? Who are you going to see? When are you going to be back?" The friend who had come to get me was a little taken aback, but my daughter was right to be concerned. In my rush to leave, I had forgotten to tell the children where I could be reached. My daughter wanted to be sure she could find me if she needed to.

Tone, attitude, and word choice are important in communicating with adolescents. "Turn that noise down" (a one-liner for which I am notorious) isn't as effective as, "Your music is too loud for me." And the latter is less critical of your adolescent's taste and judgment.

We have all been guilty of shouting, accusing, and threatening in our communications with adolescents. It would be unrealistic to deny that our interactions with them don't sometimes drive us wild. But adolescents go through some very unsettling times trying to find out who they are and where they fit in. They struggle mightily with serious questions of self and values. Their intensity is not always equaled by their tact or stability, and for these reasons they need us to stay as calm and stable as possible. A quiet firmness gives them something to lean on or push against; shouting only turns them off. It is hard to see love in an angry face or to hear respect in a raised voice. A shift in tone or choice of words can transform an accusation or a threat into a concerned question, making it more probable that it will be answered.

After yelling, criticism is the biggest complaint adolescents have about their parents. There is a place for criticism. Sometimes natural consequences aren't enough to guide your adolescent. He or she needs to be corrected, and your role is to do it. A loving tone, careful attention to word choice, and strict adherence to the subject at hand are important if your adolescent is to hear you. Sticking to the subject is hard for most people, especially if you have had to admonish your son or daughter for the same fault in the past. It is easy to bring up those other incidents, to pull in issues that are (or seem to be) related, and to keep the argument going with "and another thing. ." Easy, but not very productive. "My parents don't think I can do anything right" is a universal teenage complaint, and with good reason. Try to confine yourself to the topic at hand. If other issues need attention, they can be brought up later.

Nit-picking and nagging are closely related, and neither is an effective approach. "How are you ever going to take care of yourself?" a mother wails as her child leaves a trail of debris behind. It is appropriate to insist that the mess be picked up; speculation about the future is worse than useless. If the child has been raised in a reasonably orderly house and has been taught basic survival skills such as cooking, turning on the washing machine, and making the bed, he'll discover how useful it is to employ them regularly when he is on his own, perhaps even sooner. With little things ("Stand up straight." "Do you have to wear that color?" "Are you ever going to get your hair cut?"), it is usually better to say nothing. I have a terrible habit of correcting my children's grammar as they talk, a consequence, no doubt, of my having been an English major. My corrections are so regular, so automatic, that they scarcely seem to notice. They correct themselves without missing a beat. They are unusually good-humored about this, perhaps because I correct adults as well. More than once, they have seen my hand fly to my mouth a second after correcting my hostess, the school committee chairman, or the minister's wife. My children accept this habit of mine as a foible rather than a personal affront, but other children might not be so tolerant.

Probably the greatest concern parents have is that of communicating values and moral standards to their adolescents. They have doubtless endeavored to instill these values all through their children's lives. Now their children, on the brink of adulthood, are plunged into a world that is alien to their parents, a world of questionable heroes, a world that gives easy acceptance to alcohol, recreational drugs, and sexual experimentation. How are parents going to protect their children from experimentation that might ruin their lives?

The answer is, of course, that they cannot ensure it. Growing up means taking responsibility for your own behavior, and the prospect of this is as scary for parents as it is enticing for their children. Here is where trust comes in—trust not only in your children but also in the kind of upbringing you gave them. At this point you have to distinguish between what is your responsibility and what is your child's. You will, of course, continue to provide a good home and example; you will also ensure that your teen has access to some interesting activities and wholesome leadership. Your adolescent will have to decide whether he or she wants to take advantage of these opportunities.

You can provide your child with a safe place to explore his values aloud and with an unflappable audience for his musings. You can be ready to share your own values when he needs to hear them again, but you cannot dictate his values for him. Even if his values ultimately end up being similar to yours, he needs to think them through, to open up to the possibility of rejecting them before he can make them his own.

Finally, you can let him know that you love him through his struggles and your own. This is what communication is all about, anyway. Conducting the business of a family, talking over the day, sharing thoughts, feelings, experiences, values—they are all part of communication as well. But the bottom line, the reason we make the effort to communicate with our teenagers, is that we love them and we want them to know that. If we manage to do this, we have cleared a major hurdle and laid a foundation for a friendship with our adult children that will last a lifetime.

13

A CONVERSATION WITH MY SIXTEEN-YEAR-OLD SON

Mitch Bobrow

"I want you to get to school on time!" I shouted in my sixteen-year-old son's face. After trying every rational approach I could think of, I had finally lost my temper. Over the past eighteen months, Peter's on-time average had been roughly 60 percent. "Back when I went to high school, I *always* showed up on time. Always. I expect the same from you. Nothing less!" My anger released some of my own frustration, but it had little visible effect on Peter, whose vacant stare communicated a bored, ho-hum response.

My dilemma was a universal one. I was trying to strike the appropriate balance between too little and too much parental interference while training my teenager to act in his own best interest. Calming down, I tried another tack.

"Pete, you've been late three out of the last four days. How can I help you to be on time?"

"I don't know, Dad. Maybe you could wake me earlier."

"Come on. You're awake a good ten or fifteen minutes before you're out of bed."

"That's true. I don't like to get out of bed immediately. I like to start the day slowly."

"Very slowly." I couldn't resist the sarcasm. "Waking up is not your problem. The problem is you don't get out of bed. Maybe I should pour a little ice water on your sleepy face and chest. We'd see some action then." He knew I was bluffing, but my concern about his punctuality and seeming lack of responsibility was genuine. "Well," I said impatiently, "Tell me what's going to change."

"I'll try harder, Dad," was his instant if insincere response. We were getting nowhere. I was being humored, endured. Peter seemed to be flaunting his power. Here was a fight with his father he could win.

Photo by Michael Weisbrot

"I want to help you get to school on time. Being habitually late is a terrible habit, one that only gets harder to break as you get older."

"Dad!" Peter's exaggerated shrug cut off what he sensed might become an unwanted sermon. What teenager is inspired by a lecture? I picked up his cue and switched my tone. "I guess being on time is just not that important to you."

"I guess not." He was friendly and honest. I pressed on, missing this crucial point.

"Would it be any easier for you to get out of bed if I withdrew all your allowance for the week?"

"I don't see why that would make it easier. That would only make me angry at you."

"Well, *I* am angry that you don't get to school on time. That's your job, and you aren't successful. Your allowance comes as a recognition that you're fulfilling your responsibilities. I think taking it away might well motivate you to get to school on time."

"My allowance shouldn't be tied to school. That's unfair."

"What does fair have to do with it? I want to know if it will work."

"I don't like the idea."

"Why not? You enjoy money and the independence it offers. The loss of a few dollars might be enough to motivate you. After all, you're usually only a few minutes late. It would be very easy to get there on time." I was hoping he'd approve of my plan so the process would feel democratic, but no such luck.

"It sounds like coercion," he replied.

"It's not as if you don't have a choice, Pete. If you don't want to lose your allowance, make it your business to get to school on time. It's not coercion because you still have a choice." His sullen look said he wasn't buying my logic.

"Then you propose something," I said.

"I'll try harder," he retorted, more in anger than commitment.

"That's not good enough. If you can't come up with a better plan, then starting this week, you lose your allowance if you are late even one day during the week."

Fall slowly became winter. I watched and said little. My teenager's routine hardly varied. Awake at seven. Out of bed at seven-fifteen and into the shower. Dressed and downstairs by seven-forty. Breakfast eaten and lunch prepared by eight. Out the door by five after. Too bad school started at five after and was a ten-minute walk from home.

Three months later, I was $40 richer but sorry for it. It was time for another conversation. "Cutting your allowance is not working. True, you're doing a little better. You made it to school on time for several weeks, but in general you're still late a lot."

"I know. I told you docking my allowance was a lousy idea." Pete seemed a trifle amused.

"We need a different strategy," I admitted. I myself had been out of solutions for some time now. "Any ideas?" I wondered.

"No," he replied.

"Me neither." We were stuck, not an unfamiliar experience. As a therapist, I knew that impasses occur frequently in the growth process. My job at such times is to reconnect my clients to their original intentions. It was time to apply the same lesson at home. I needed to touch base with Peter.

"Do you want to get to school on time?" Peter paused for a while, contemplating this basic question.

"I do. I don't like being late," he tentatively began. "At the same time, I do well in school, and it doesn't seem like such a big deal if I'm a few minutes late now and then. It's just one class."

"So your intention is to get to school on time if you can, and if you can't, not to worry about it."

"I guess." His attitude was consistent with his 60 percent on-time average. "It's not that important, Dad. You want me to be honest, don't you? My first period teacher gets a little upset when I show up late, but I still do well in the class. I'm not her biggest problem."

"This helps. I'm glad you can admit that it's not that important to you. We both know that you could make it to school on time if you wanted to."

It began to dawn on me that I was the one with the problem. He didn't care. "I must be missing something," I reflected out loud, my mood shifting. "What would you do if you were the father in this situation? How would you try to motivate your kid?"

Peter thought for a while and cockily said, "Why not try positive reinforcement? If I get to school on time, give me a bonus. You could double my allowance. That might get me up earlier, you know. Positive instead of negative reinforcement."

"A bonus for behavior that's already expected of you? No thanks."

"It might motivate me faster than punishment."

"Your younger brother already gets to school on time. If I give you a bonus, he'll want one, too. Rewards are for actions above and beyond the call of duty, and this isn't one of those."

"Well, I think it could work."

"Something is missing, Pete, and I can't figure out what. You are obviously quite responsible in just about every other area of your life. I trust you to be honest; you're kind and cooperative; you do well in school; so much of your life is working. Usually you're a pleasure to be around. I don't understand why you can't get to school on time." My mood had shifted. I recognized that I had no control in this situation. My initial anger was replaced by a growing sadness.

Thinking slowly, Peter responded, "It's not that important to me. I understand that it matters to you, but you have never convinced me why this is important. I am doing well in school anyway. I'm not learning any less."

"But it sets up a precedent—a bad habit that gets you in the mode of not being on time, and I don't think you'll be able to snap out of it when you need to." He was unimpressed.

What could I do? Take away a privilege like his skiing? Ground him? I was trying to instill responsibility, and I knew that punishment would only foster resentment and anger. Besides, I wanted him to want to get to school on time and he didn't care. Defeat stared me in the face. Short of picking him up and carrying him to school, I was powerless.

"I guess I lose, Pete." My sad acceptance of defeat surprised him. "There's nothing I can say or do to get you to be on time. I won't bug you about it anymore." I walked out of his room.

Sinking into my rocking chair, I settled sadly to reflect on what had happened. It was time to relinquish more parental responsibility, an inherently healthy if painful process. How common to offer either too little or too much slack as the growing child gropes toward independence. Today's message was clear: it's his job, not mine, to get to school on time. If I haven't instilled a desire for responsibility by now, it's too late.

About three minutes after I sat down, Peter came looking for me. Now he was upset. Our conversation had unnerved him. It was totally out of character for me to walk out of a disagreement sadly throwing my hands up in defeat.

"I didn't think we were done. I don't understand why you walked out," he said. I was surprised that he wanted to continue. Now we

Photo by Michael Weisbrot

were both out of character. He was initiating a discussion about his own shortcomings.

"What more is there to say?" I wondered.

"You haven't convinced me why I should get to school on time."

"I didn't think I could. You had all the answers."

"If it's so important to you, how come you can't convince me?"

"Good question." His perseverance was impressive. He seemed suddenly older and more mature. He was approaching this conversation without the haughtiness or joviality that had only ten minutes ago been so obvious. His intent had shifted.

Groping at first for words, I said. "Well, I'm glad you came back to talk. I guess we should start at the beginning and go over this again." I took a minute or two to feel out my problem. "I think your lateness upsets me because it feels somehow like you are lying—violating your own agreement—not playing by the rules. Sometimes when I get on the open highway on a sunny day with no traffic, I want to drive seventy or even eighty miles an hour. But I don't. I honor and respect the basic rules of the road. I'm glad there's a speed limit and an enforcement of that limit. It makes driving safer. I wouldn't trust a law that invited all drivers to use their own discretion about how fast they could safely travel. It wouldn't work. Ground rules are needed. Similarly, if kids showed up at school whenever they felt like it, the school system would be a farce. I think your school has a right to ask you to come at a certain time. When you ignore that guideline, you're taking the law into your own hands. I don't trust people who think they are above the law."

"Gee, Dad, you're saying I'm untrustworthy because I show up five minutes late for English a couple of times a week? Give me a break."

"Suppose I didn't keep even 10 percent of the agreements I made with you. Would you trust me? If you expect me to take you to the movies and I space it out or show up late, that would certainly affect our relationship. Besides, whose rule is it that you must be at school at five after eight?"

"School policy."

"I know that, but do you think a school system needs to create such a policy and such a restriction?"

"Obviously they do."

"Do you have a choice about going to school?" The question surprised both of us. Peter had turned sixteen only last week. For the first time he now had the option of quitting. School was no longer a requirement but a choice.

"I don't think of school as a choice. It's something I've always done, always expected to do."

"Maybe that's the problem. You've inherited your education rather than chosen it. But something is different now. This is a conversation we could not have had two weeks ago. Sixteen is a significant age. It's the beginning of adulthood. Commit a serious crime and you're no longer treated as a juvenile. You're eligible to drive, and you can drop out of school. Last week you had no choice about school. This week you do. Although I know you don't plan to drop out, still, your status has changed. You are there by choice, whether you own that choice or ignore it. Do you understand the significance of this?"

He looked intrigued. "Not completely," he said. "Keep going."

"If school is a real bona fide choice, then you need to examine what your agreements are. Instead of thinking about the rules as something forced on you, you can now look upon them as guidelines that you respect. You've already agreed that school wouldn't work if kids showed up whenever they felt like it. Getting to school on time is a rule that makes education possible. It's a rule you'd want everyone who values their education to abide by. The problem is that you can get away with breaking it. Your teacher gives you a dirty look and that's that. But every time you get away with breaking the rule, you cheapen the rule and ultimately confuse yourself."

"By giving yourself permission to be randomly late, you set yourself up as the maker of the rules. You've taken the law into your own hands, which sets you apart from others and from the community. I am speaking theoretically here because in all practicality there are no consequences for showing up a little late. But I think there's a hidden danger with definite consequences when you're late, and that's why I'm making such an issue about this. Life is difficult enough without having to examine which rules to keep and which to amend. Our mind bogs down when we have too many decisions to make. Each morning you have to decide: should I get up now or later? Is it okay to be late today? How tired am I? You're overworking your mind, keeping it distracted with petty decisions. Am I making sense?"

Peter looked interested. "Are you saying that when I come late to school, I'm breaking my own rule?"

"Exactly. And look at the ramifications of that. How can you trust yourself if you break your own rules? Your aunt told me that she lied a lot when she was a kid. That was not a problem for her, but one day she found herself believing her own bullshit. That freaked her out, and she stopped lying altogether. How can you trust yourself if you don't know what behaviors to expect from yourself? Your self-esteem and self-worth relate to being honest and straight with yourself. If you have an agreement to be on time, and you ignore that agreement whenever you don't feel like keeping it, you open yourself to a nightmare of confusion and uncertainty."

Peter simply listened. I was not sure how much he was absorbing, but his look invited me to continue.

"Every time you break your own rule, you have less power and less confidence. I want you to be a powerful person, someone who has as much control over life as possible. Getting to school on time is not the real issue. The issue is trusting yourself and taking responsibility for the choices you make in life. This may be a little difficult to grasp. Adulthood, thankfully, comes on gradually. You go from being taken care of to taking care of yourself. You've seen the relay races where the baton is passed from one member of the team to the next. Adolescence is like life in the passing zone. At first you run alongside your teammate without the baton. Then comes the handoff. It must be smooth or precious time is lost. Then you're on your own. At sixteen the handoff is just beginning. You have several more years of running by my side as I pass more and more responsibility over to you. I look forward to it. Once you take off on your own, it means at last that we can become friends in addition to being father and son."

Peter looked at me and smiled. Then he gave me a long warm hug. This morning as I glanced out the window, I saw my son running up our steep driveway. It was two minutes to eight. He was late, but by running he'd make it on time.

14

WHAT TEENAGERS WANT
FROM ADULTS

Susannah Sheffer

Sometimes our popular beliefs about teenagers so color our attitudes toward them that it becomes difficult for us to think about certain important questions that concern them. What do teenagers want from the adults in their lives? How can those adults be most helpful? We know that teenagers are often rebellious and immersed in their own subculture and that there is often a great gulf between young people and adults. When we think of stereotypical teenagers, it can easily appear as if what teenagers want most from adults is to be left alone.

At *Growing Without Schooling*, the magazine about home education and children's learning of which I am editor, we often hear from teenagers. For one issue, we asked several teenagers to write specifically about what they wanted from adults. These young people aren't typical, most obviously because they don't go to school. They may, therefore, be less invested in what we think of as the youth culture than others their age and more likely to see themselves as already part of the adult world. Nevertheless, I don't think these teenagers form such an exclusive group that it is impossible to learn from them. There is much in what they say that applies to all.

The letters of these adolescents suggest that teenagers want courtesy and honesty from their elders and access to the adult world. These sound like basic things to want from other people, but teenagers are having a hard time getting them.

Of the three, courtesy is perhaps the easiest to give and also the easiest to forget to give. The late educator John Holt often told a story about a student he taught during the 1960s at a small, private, evening high school. Many of the students there were inner city kids who had not been successful at other schools. The mother of one boy told

Photo by Jill Fineberg

John that she had asked her son why he liked this school so much. At first he could not come up with an answer, but after a while he blurted out, "Listen, Mom, I've been going to school for eleven years now, and this is the first time anyone has ever said 'Please' to me!" Amazing that such respect should be so rare, but it *is* rare, in our dealings with young children as well as in our dealings with teenagers. We underestimate how much difference even small courtesies make to people who are used to being bossed around and having their feelings ignored. Of course, without a deeper courtesy underlying these words, the words themselves will eventually wear thin. But the words are a beginning.

When teenagers talk about wanting honesty from adults, they are talking above all about wanting adults to be themselves around teenagers, to reveal their real attitudes, fears, and biases rather than posing as generic authority figures. A thirteen-year-old boy told us that when he is "treated as an ignoramus" in conversation with an adult, he not only gets annoyed and frustrated but also doesn't "gain anything because [he] can never get a decent response." By a "decent response" this boy means an answer to whatever question he might have asked, but I think he also means an answer that reflects the particular attitudes and beliefs of the adult responding. In other words, the boy wants an answer that reveals a bit of that adult and thus gives him something to work with as he decides what kind of adult he would like to be. Honest responses allow young people a glimpse of the range of possibilities in adult life and help them to imagine their own choices.

Giving access can be as simple as making adult lives and activities visible to teenagers. When my fifteen-year-old friend Kim told me she was interested in how the law works, we went to watch a trial at the local courthouse. Kim had known that she was interested in the law, but she didn't know what to do next. She had not known that most trials are open to the public. By showing her that this aspect of adult society was in fact more accessible than she had realized, I helped make something visible that had been invisible before. In the same way, when I show Kim and the other young writers I work with drafts of my own writing and tell them a bit about the process of work behind the finished product, I am letting them see that aspect of the working adult world.

Just when young people seem to be growing more independent of us and more able to do things on their own (we no longer think in terms of "child care" when it comes to teenagers), they may in fact need our help in new and very specific ways. When she was beginning to consider ways of getting involved in work or apprenticeships outside her home, Kim wrote to me:

> For a long time, I was content to just go about, doing whatever I felt like. Now the things I want to do have to be planned, and often involve getting other people to help. . . . Mom and I have spent a lot of time working on this together. We're kind of forming a new relationship now—before, she wasn't participating in my life much. I was off by myself a lot, writing, reading, whatever. Now I feel I would like her to be more involved—not because I need someone to lead me but because I want someone to help me find ways to do the things I want to do.

"Help me find ways to do the things I want to do" is a perfect summary of what teenagers most want from adults. Often the things adolescents want to do involve the adult world more than they did in earlier years, which is why adult help becomes especially necessary. Anna-Lisa Cox, a seventeen-year-old who wrote to *Growing Without Schooling* about her love of social anthropology and history—specifically, the study of antique clothing—went on to say that she would now like to work with a museum curator who could help her pursue her interest further. "It's true that most major museums offer internships," Anna-Lisa wrote,

> but the ones they set up for teenagers are usually very mundane—being a cashier at the museum store or running errands. They only offer the specific kind of internship I am looking for to graduate students or professionals. This is frustrating for me because I have come to the point in my studies of antique clothing where I am looking at a very specialized area, as specialized as any graduate student's. Yet because of my age I do not have a chance to work with someone willing to help me.
>
> One way in which adults can be very helpful to young people is in opening doors. Getting past the "front desk" is almost impossible for me. All adults see is the number seventeen, and they slam the door in my face. It's not fair that I'm not even given the chance to prove myself.

Adult help at the right time can make all the difference between fulfillment and frustration. Fourteen-year-old Carey Newman, a serious artist, described how his mother helped him apply to an art school that didn't normally accept anyone under sixteen. Thirteen-year-old Amanda Bergson-Shilcock wrote about taking a spinning course with her younger sister; they were the only young people in the class. She said, "We really enjoyed and appreciated the fact that everybody in the group accepted us, as if we belonged there. At the same time, I think it was a little unfair that the course was open to adults only, so any adult could get in, but we had to prove ourselves."

Wanting to pursue their interests in antique clothing, or art, or spinning, these young people recognize that they often need adult help to get past the barriers that society has put up between them and the things they want to do. They need, in a sense, an adult advocate and navigator. To use another metaphor, they need a travel agent, someone who can outline for them the various ways to get where they want to go and can help them decide which way is best. Then, when they actually take the trip, they may need people to welcome them at various points along the way.

Why is it so hard for us to give teenagers what they clearly tell us they want from us? Part of it has to do with the way we think about adolescence in the first place. The teenagers who wrote to *Growing Without Schooling* know that adolescence has a terrible reputation and that one of their chief tasks is simply overcoming that negative image. One wrote, "When I turned thirteen, the thing I worried about most was that I would suddenly be considered a confused and frivolous teenager." Another wrote, "There is a popular belief that teenagers are antisocial creatures for whom responsibility is a dirty word."

Indeed, there may be no other stage of life about which our general expectations are as firmly and as overwhelmingly negative. We seem to fear the tenuousness of adolescence, the fact that so much is at stake and so much could go wrong. We worry that young people will be led down dangerous paths while they are still vulnerable, prefer recklessness to responsibility, and, perhaps most important, fail to fit themselves into the adult world in a way that they, and we, can be proud of.

Some of our fears may be generated by the reckless or antisocial behavior that some teenagers do engage in. But to what extent is a group responsible for its own image? The convenience store near my office posts a sign near its magazine rack that says: "No loitering by teenagers." Now, it may indeed be teenagers who have given this store

Photo by Michael Weisbrot

its loitering problem. But would we ever, in this day and age, post a sign that said: "No loitering by blacks"? It is destructive and insulting to anyone to be seen, above all else, as part of a class. This is what the teenagers in *Growing Without Schooling* were objecting to when they wrote about having to overcome their age group's negative image.

And yet, ironically, this negative image is constantly contradicted. We assume adolescence is a difficult time, but we also romanticize youth in many ways. We accuse teenagers of being immature and in the next breath warn them not to grow up too fast. We urge them to accept responsibility but envy them for being so carefree. More than anything else, our culture seems to be *confused* about teenagers, and I think that this actually reflects our misgivings about adulthood. Is adulthood a burdensome time of life, laden with responsibility and pressure, from which we look back in envy at the fun of adolescence? Or is adulthood a time in which we are in many ways freer, surer of ourselves and of our place in the world, than we were as teenagers? How we feel about adulthood affects how we feel about teenagers. It determines the extent to which, and the way in which, we welcome them into the adult world.

Paul Goodman wrote in his book, *Growing Up Absurd* (published in the mid-1950s, but no less true today) that young people's biggest problem was the society in which they were expected to grow up. "The question is," Goodman wrote, "what it means to grow up into such a fact as: During my productive years I will spend eight hours a day doing what is no good." If adult work is boring, trivial, wasteful, destructive, or any of the other negative things that adults may feel and teenagers may perceive it to be, how can teenagers look forward to a time when they will have to spend most of their waking lives at that work? If the adult world is meaningless, dishonest, phony— things teenagers have accused it of being—how can teenagers even begin to think about finding their place in that world? Because adolescence is not a permanent condition, because its central task is finding ways to move outward into the world, the problems of teenagers are inextricably bound up with the problems of the adult world that awaits them.

But why talk about teenagers moving into the wider world when it so often appears as if teenagers want anything *but* adult society? Stereotypical teenagers, with their own clothing, hairstyles, music, heroes, and values, may seem so unconnected to the adult society they are bound for that it is foolish to talk about the relationship between the two.

Yet this relationship is crucial. We have to consider the ways in which we drive teenagers into this stereotypical subculture by leaving it the only culture available to them. Young people make the relatively narrow world of traditional adolescence their whole world because they are denied meaningful participation anywhere else.

In thinking about why young people become interested in smoking and drinking, John Holt suggested that the lure of these activities may be that they are among the few adult activities genuinely available to teenagers. If we assume that young people want to grow up—and I cannot believe that the job of a healthy young person would be anything other than continued growth and increasing competence—we have to realize that they will do what they can. If meaningful work and active participation in adult society are unavailable to them, they will take what is available, which is usually the *trappings* of adulthood, its superficial habits and behaviors. Conversely, the teenagers I know who seem least interested in these trappings—and who may therefore look or seem younger on the surface—have a greater genuine connection to the adult world (real friends who are adults, an understanding of how some parts of the adult world work, a chance to help adults do important things, and so on) than do most of their peers.

This is not to say that this is all there is to the problems of teenage smoking, drinking, and drug use. Much contributes to them, not the least of which is our own confusion about these habits. We haven't resolved or made peace with our own dependence, as individuals and as a society, on these substances, and perhaps we resent teenagers for mirroring our confusion. But it is important to look at which aspects of the adult world we give teenagers access to and which we deny them. Perhaps if teenagers have genuine, active, interesting ways to move into and ultimately join adult society, they will be less likely to resort to trivial or destructive ways.

The adults who can be most helpful to teenagers in this respect are adults who truly like being adults and like the work they do. If I like my work, I will think it is worth showing to young people and I will make the effort to do so. If I truly feel that adulthood is worth sticking around for, I may be able to persuade a young person of this and help him or her avoid a total retreat into the youth subculture. But if I don't feel either of these things, I'm not going to be of much real use to teenagers. If we want to think about teenagers, then, we have to think about adults as well. One of the great tasks of adolescence is to figure out what one wants adulthood to be like and what one will do when one gets there.

15

PREVENTING AND SOLVING THE ALCOHOL AND DRUG PROBLEMS OF TEENAGERS

Robert Schwebel

"Why do you smoke so much pot?" I asked the fifteen-year-old girl. She had been referred to my office because of serious school, drug, and now legal problems.

"Because being high is the only way I can stand going to school. Because it's the only way I can stand being around my parents. Because everything's more fun when I'm high. Because all my friends smoke pot. We drink beer, too. We like it."

This articulate teenager knew how she felt. And if you think about it, her reasons for using alcohol and pot closely resemble the reasons that many adults consume these same drugs and other psychoactive substances: to relieve stress; to have fun; to feel good; to conform with their peers. Small surprise that we have a drug problem with our youth when you consider the extent to which *adults* in our culture consume legal and illegal substances to cope with stress in their lives and to serve as a remedy to their psychological and health problems.

Another factor contributing to juvenile drug use has been the permissive message that until recently we implicitly communicated to young people concerning alcohol and other drugs. It went something like this: "We will say to you on an *official* level not to use drugs. But you can use them as long as you don't get into trouble. If you keep out of trouble, we'll look the other way."

Our reason for this permissive message was that social and economic changes that started in the 1950s and 1960s put new pressures on parents. With more women in the paid work force and increasing numbers of single parent families, many parents had less time for their children. They were simply too busy. Another reason was that the parents of today's children were largely unaware of the dangers of drugs. During their childhood twenty and thirty years ago, they were

Photo by Michael Weisbrot

exposed to scare tactics, in which drug dangers were grossly exaggerated. Not surprisingly, they discounted this preposterous propaganda but were left basically uninformed about the *real* dangers.

The permissive message to children about alcohol and other drugs proved to be a surefire setup for trouble. Allowing children and young teenagers to freely use powerful substances inevitably resulted in problems. The outcome is that now we have a drug problem with our youth.

As a society, have we faced the problem squarely? I would say not yet. The major governmental emphasis has been on interdiction and cutting supply. This approach is doomed to fail, because new drugs and new suppliers always appear. Meanwhile, support for treatment has been inadequate. We still have long waiting lists of addicted individuals who want to break their drug habit but cannot find or afford a program. In terms of prevention, we have reverted to scare tactics that have already been proven ineffective. The banner now of government leaders who want to prevent substance abuse is "Just Say No," an approach that has proved helpful in some ways but that does not deal with the underlying causes of drug abuse.

The "Say No" slogan delivers a new and clear message from adults to young people: Drugs are not for children. Note the message is not "only adults can use drugs," because that statement makes drug use seem like a sign of maturity. Because drugs are powerful substances that can interfere with healthy development, I believe it is important that parents communicate this "no use" message to children. It is also important that children learn to resist negative peer pressure, and "Just Say No" has been helpful in that regard. But the idea that drug use can be prevented simply by teaching children to utter a slogan is much too simplistic. With teenagers, it is developmentally inappropriate. This age group is making the transition from childhood to adulthood. Instead of being told to parrot a slogan, teens need to be given opportunities to think for themselves and to work on forming their own independent identities.

A serious flaw of a prevention strategy based on urging children to resist peer pressure ("saying no") is that it does not deal with the root causes of drug abuse. Explaining the drug use of children on the basis of their inability to resist peer pressure is circular reasoning. Why does one child use drugs? Because all the other ones do. But then, who started it? And why do so many children use drugs in the first place? Our national prevention efforts do not address these important, basic questions.

If we want to understand the root causes of drug abuse, as well as the potential solutions, we need to consider seriously what teenagers, such as the fifteen-year-old quoted at the beginning of this essay, have to say. They are using alcohol and other drugs to meet their needs. If we want our children to be free from the perils of drug problems, then we must teach them the attitudes and skills that will enable them to take care of themselves. Drug prevention is health promotion. It means empowering children to meet their needs in healthy ways.

Health promotion begins long before children have access to alcohol and other drugs. It includes teaching young children to think clearly, to maintain good relationships, to have positive values about themselves and others, and to make good decisions. It includes teaching them how to cope with stress without drugs, how to plan recreation, excitement, and pleasure without drugs, and how to solve problems without drugs.

Do busy parents, under significant stress themselves, have the time, energy, and ability to empower their children? If they don't, the drug problem and a wide variety of other behavioral problems will persist, no matter how many times we tell children to "Just Say No." It's a question of spending time now in an active, positive way to prevent problems, or spending enormous amounts of time later reacting to the tragic consequences of neglect.

One argument I often hear when I conduct parent workshops is that parents are being too nice with their teenage children. We need to stop this "education business" and get tough: lay down the law. Teens will obey our rules or else face severe consequences for misbehavior. Children must do as they are told. This is what I call the authoritarian approach. It sounds so simple and seems so convenient for today's tired and busy parents. However, the problem is that it doesn't work with healthy teenagers trying hard to think for themselves and to forge their own independent identities. More than anything else, the authoritarian approach breeds rebellion, as in the following exchange.

Dad: "I don't ever want to hear about you using drugs. If you use them, you're out of the house."

Son: "Don't worry, Dad. You won't ever *hear* about it."

And so the dialogue ends, and parents lose their most important power, the educational influence. And if children are not talking with parents about drugs, then they will get all their information from peers and the mass media. That, in my opinion, is risky business.

Parents are rightfully concerned about their teenagers using drugs. But slogans and authoritarian gestures are not solutions to the problem. It is through an educational approach that parents can maximize their influence and make a difference. The challenge of working with teenagers is in engaging them in dialogue and helping them learn to think for themselves and to make wise choices. Through dialogue, parents and teenagers can establish mutual understanding and make clear and valid agreements. When agreements are broken, parents can respond constructively to promote further understanding and growth in their children. All of this is done with proper parental supervision and authority but with an eye toward empowering the young adult. I call this type of dialogue the exchange of information process. It has five components: (1) opening the dialogue; (2) parents saying what they think and feel about drugs; (3) children expressing their point of view; (4) parents and children talking together and making agreements; and (5) parents watching to see how the agreements are working.

To some people, a dialogue approach sounds quite permissive and perhaps overly democratic. These people confuse discussion with surrender. Dialogue increases mutual understanding and respect in the family. Parents who talk with their children do not surrender their authority and can continue to set a high standard of behavior.

Opening the Dialogue
The first step in the exchange of information process is to create a very special home atmosphere that allows for an open dialogue in which any topic can be discussed without fear.

You can find out quickly if you have such an environment by asking your teenager, in a nonthreatening way, "Can we talk about drugs?" If the answer is "No," or an insincere "Yeah, sure (let's get it over with)," then, before you can start discussing drugs, you need to work on the family climate. Children must feel that they can speak their mind without being punished. They need to feel that you will listen and seriously consider their point of view.

As parents, you have to insist on the importance of a discussion, but you may need to backtrack to diagnose the obstacles. The basic question is, "What do we need to do to make you (the teenager) feel safe enough to talk with us (the parents)?" Sometimes this calls for serious self-criticism by parents and a commitment to change some bad habits, such as overreliance on punishment or a tendency to lecture. One parent put it this way, "You told me you don't want to talk because I lecture you. I think you're right; I do have a tendency to lecture. But we must discuss drugs at home. Drugs are a reality in our world, and I want to help prepare you for this challenge. I want to stop the lecture business. You're too old for that stuff. I won't do it anymore. But we need to talk and listen to each other."

Exchanging Points of View

After the opening of the dialogue comes the back-and-forth exchange of points of view. To participate in an educational exchange, you will need to be informed yourself. You don't have to be a drug expert (and you can always use references when you are confused), but a basic understanding of types of drugs and their effects is a good starting point. Don't forget tobacco and nicotine. Tobacco is highly addictive, socially accepted by many, one of the first drugs used by children, and a serious health hazard.

Getting the facts is the easy part. It is somewhat more difficult to clarify values. In other words, much of what we think about drugs is not as much fact as it is opinion. In preparing for a discussion, it helps to think through your point of view on drugs and to be prepared to explain why, for example, you would consider certain types of drug-taking behavior acceptable (i.e., adults who do not have a drinking problem having a glass of wine with dinner) and other types unacceptable.

Then it is important to be a good listener. I warn first against what I call "conversation stoppers": threats or pronouncements that tend to close the dialogue. I have heard parents say, "Anyone who even thinks about smoking pot is a total jerk." This clearly would put an end to discussion in many homes. I also suggest parents try to avoid the rebuttal cycle, wherein everything a teenager says is immediately challenged.

Parents become good teachers and fully use the power of their educational influence when they help raise the consciousness of their children. This means you do not overpower children with your own ideas. Instead, you listen to your children, help them to broaden and expand their thinking, and help them find the contradictions within their own thought processes.

Photo by John Schoenwalter Photography

Almost all young children who have been raised with positive attitudes and taught basic life skills will agree not to use drugs if their parents give them a clear message about the health risks. The same can be said about some teenagers, but not all of them. The teenage years are a time when children experiment. They are very interested in body sensations. Some teenagers, in their efforts to establish an independent identity, will try alcohol and other drugs over the objections of their parents.

This is when the educational power of parents is so important. It is also when parents often panic and blunder by overreacting. The challenge is to get those children who have used drugs to think carefully about what they are doing, how it has affected them, and how it might affect them in the future.

The questions parents will want to answer for themselves are:

1. What drugs? What quantity? How often?

2. What is the motivation for drug use?

3. What has been the impact—immediate and cumulative—of the drug use?

4. What is your child's attitude about drug use?

5. Is your child informed about drugs? Does your child have self-awareness about the impact and risks of his or her drug use?

6. What is the current status of drug use? Has it stopped? Will he or she use them if they are available? Is the teenager actively looking for drugs? Parents may discover that a child who has tried alcohol or pot has already quit. The drug use may have been a one-shot affair.

By calmly gathering this information in a discussion, parents give their children a chance to think these questions through for themselves. This is when the art of parent-as-educator reaches its highest form. Lots of open-ended questions are important, such as, "How was it?" This is preferable to questions that lead to one-word answers such as, "Did you like it?" "Who were you with?" "Are you going to do it again?" Remember, you don't want to scare or cross-examine your children. You want to open a dialogue to get them thinking.

When your children seem unclear, you can help with some directed questioning. For example, if they don't understand their motivation for drug use, you can say, "Let's go back and see what was happening last time you smoked pot. What was the situation?"

"Well, it was last Saturday night. I was with Mark and Larry. We were bored."

"Oh, do you think maybe sometimes you smoke pot because you're bored?"

"Yeah, I guess maybe."

The process of drawing children out and then making observations about what they say is a powerful educational approach. For example, a teenager who says he could quit smoking pot whenever he wants is asked if he has ever tried.

"Yes. I've stopped."

"But then you started again?"

"Yeah, my teachers were hassling me in school."

"So it sounds like you have some control. You can stop for a while. But when the pressure gets intense, you start again. Does that sound right?"

"Yes, but I was really being hassled."

"Okay, I understand you were under stress."

Notice the parent in this example doesn't dwell on the point. By backing off at this moment, he leaves the child thinking about the connection that has just been made.

Sometimes what I call "thought-provoking questions" are helpful. This involves asking children if they have ever considered the flip side or opposite of what they are saying. I asked a sixteen-year-old girl who was marveling about the wonders of alcohol to consider the flip side.

"Is there another side to this? Have you ever worried about your alcohol use?"

Taken aback by my nonthreatening tone, she admitted some trepidation. I didn't need to provide information. She knew the down side of her alcohol use, and I helped her think about it one more time.

Making Agreements

After having a dialogue, agreements are made. They can be based on a shared understanding ("We see things the same way"); respect for parental authority ("We differ, but I ask that you agree to my terms"); compromise ("We meet each other halfway"); or parental power ("Agree to my terms or the consequences will be. . ."). A valid agreement is crystal clear, understood by all, and accepted by all. Agreements that are not fully understood or accepted probably will be broken.

Most younger teenagers will agree to parental prohibitions when it comes to alcohol or other drug use. With this age group, I believe parents must insist that children stop using drugs. Many older teenagers who have been treated respectfully will also agree to parental terms. Some are already anxious about drugs, are relieved their parents have started a discussion, and quickly decide to discontinue their drug use. But some will argue that they are using alcohol or other drugs responsibly, just as some adults do. My belief is that childhood (or adolescence) is not a healthy time to be using drugs, and adults should oppose drug use. But adults also must be realistic. Any child old enough to climb out a window, to drive a car, or to go to a high school can gain access to drugs.

Sometimes a single, serious jolt of consequence from parents will force teenagers to think over what they're doing and to stop using drugs. Those teens might be anxious themselves about their drug use. However, in many instances, punishment interrupts drug use in the short run but encourages it in the long haul. Teenagers stop because they are scared but will start again when they feel stronger or more rebellious.

The key issue is assessing harm. If harm is imminent or already occurring (drunken or drugged driving, failure in school, trouble with the law, use of highly addictive drugs such as crack, etc.), then parents can trade off their educational influence in return for immediate, strong intervention, with the hope of reopening a dialogue later. However, if the drug use is only mild, parents can temporarily tolerate it, while using their educational influence to gradually help their children understand the potential dangers. In the long run this is effective, because teenagers end up fully aware of what they are doing, the effects of their drug use, and the risks.

I realize that to say this these days is almost sacrilegious. The prevalent point of view is that parents should virtually chain their teenagers to the wall to stop them from using drugs. But I think this is wishful thinking instead of logical problem solving. Too many people in this country are looking for a quick fix, an easy solution, to a complex problem. They think that an authoritarian attitude and repressive punishment will "win the war against drugs."

Instead of pounding our chests and making threats, we should invest our energy in educating our children and helping them to become powerful and healthy individuals who can make wise decisions for themselves. Smart, powerful teenagers with self-respect will not abuse alcohol or other drugs. We should also be role models of what we want to teach our teenagers. We are teaching self-control; we need to model self-control. We are teaching children to face the stress of life without relying on simplistic, ineffective solutions; we need to do this ourselves. We are teaching problem solving. We are teaching respect. In our efforts, in our own families, we can set wonderful examples.

16

WHEN YOUR CHILD IS
TROUBLED

Elizabeth Hormann

When Sally was a young woman, she worked as a lab technician. Although she enjoyed her job, she had no pangs about leaving when her baby came along. She loved mothering him and also the little sister who joined him a couple of years later. Full-time mothering and homemaking suited her and met the needs of her children right through the grade school years. Returning to work at that point served her family's changing needs—and her own.

Sally's daughter was a high school sophomore when her behavior began to change. She cried constantly, resisted going to school, and begged her mother to stay home. When her daughter's distress became overwhelming, Sally took a leave of absence. She also got some professional help, and it was then that she learned about the emotional illness that would be with her daughter for a lifetime. "When I was a younger mother, I was not very tolerant of families who had trouble with their children," says Sally. "I could always point to deficiencies in parenting that 'caused' the problems. But I've learned better. You can love your children, do your best to bring them up to be healthy and happy, and *still* something like this can happen."

Maggie expected good results from her mothering, too. "I birthed at home, nursed each child for two or three years, and tried to help them grow at their own pace," she recalls. "With the first two, I really believed I had done it. They are terrific, outgoing, interesting people. They did well in school and have sensible plans for the future. Our third child looked like he would follow right along, but when he hit thirteen, all hell broke loose. He became cocky, loud, and hostile. He skipped school to go drinking with his buddies. Drugs followed hard on the liquor. He failed the same grade twice. We tried frantically to help him get his behavior under control, but we finally had to admit

Photo by Lloyd Wolf

that we couldn't do it alone.

"Hard as it was, we admitted him to a private psychiatric hospital. He fought therapy, and he fought our visits; but we persisted, and he got better. He didn't like the idea of a special school, but we insisted, and the year he spent there changed his life—and ours. To this day, we cannot explain why he was vulnerable in ways our other children were not, but we are grateful there were people to help us through that near-disastrous time."

Healthy Families and Troubled Children

It is a well-kept secret that good families can have troubled children. According to the National Institute of Mental Health, in 1988, the number of American children suffering from mental illnesses such as anxiety, depression, schizophrenia, and the effects of drug abuse was 9.5 million. Society likes to blame these problems on poor parenting. Parents themselves do it; members of the helping professions have adopted it as an article of faith; even television scripts paint parents as the villains when their children are in trouble.

A film on teen suicide portrays this vividly. One set of parents shows little interest in their child; she attempts suicide and is hospitalized. When she is released, they pretend nothing has happened. The father in the second family orchestrates his son's life so completely and holds himself up as a model of such virtue that when his secret love affair accidentally comes to light, his son becomes shattered to the point of suicide.

Of course, it sometimes happens that parents *are* at the root of their children's problems. Very often, however, they are not entirely responsible for them; and in other instances, they may not be responsible at all. Children come into the world with unique personalities and needs. Some children are needier and more vulnerable than others. All children are subject to influences other than their parents, and most children lack the consistent good judgment that can always keep them out of trouble.

As new parents, we do not like to consider the possibility of our well-loved children traveling a rocky path to adulthood. We want assurance that our efforts will make a difference; that careful attention to the youngster's needs will pay off in an older child who is not prey to the temptations of drugs, alcohol, and early sexual involvement, and who does not develop school phobias or eating disorders, or get

into trouble with the law. But nurturing in the early years cannot
guarantee smooth sailing later on. What good parenting gives our
children is a running start in life, not lifelong immunity from difficulties. A troubled child still can—and often does—crop up in a family
that is fundamentally happy and healthy.

In her book *Traits of a Healthy Family*, Dolores Curran reports on a
survey taken among family life professionals to uncover just what
those traits might be. Freedom from problems was not one of them.
However, healthy families *did* know how to recognize problems and
get help when they needed it. What distinguished healthy families
from less healthy ones was a willingness to work on their problems.

A troubled child in a healthy family has a good chance of recovery
because the foundation is so well laid. The basic stability and ties of
affection that hold the family together contribute to an enhanced
perspective—enabling the family to see not only that there is a problem but that their child's trouble is only one aspect of their lives. The
healthy family can thus move quickly past the stages of asking why or
laying blame and begin to work on solutions.

When and Where to Seek Help

Figuring out the problem is the first step in solving it. Sometimes it is
easy to see what is wrong: the child may be failing in school or skip-
ping it altogether, using drugs or alcohol, or acting out sexually or in
ways that attract attention from the law. But very often, children are
"not themselves" in ways that are hard to pin down. They may show
physical symptoms—a large weight loss or gain; excessive sleep, or too
little of it; or perhaps a "drawn" look. They may become furiously
active or quietly withdrawn. Children signal when something is
wrong.

It can be tempting to overlook both the subtle and the not-so-
subtle cues. After all, we are aware that most youngsters do skip
school or experiment with drugs or act out in unpleasant ways at
some time during their childhood careers, and we are careful not to
overreact. Nevertheless, children need *some* reaction to these
behaviors. They need to know that their actions matter, both now
and for the future. They need to know that their feelings matter. And
they need to know that we will try to help them alter an upsetting situation, or at least offer ongoing support as they struggle through it.
Occasional acting out can usually be handled within the family; but

when it becomes more than occasional, it is time to find a professional helper.

A good helper can provide not only a clear analysis of what is causing the problem but also some concrete assistance in solving it. Unfortunately, and ironically, it is not always easy to find a good mental health professional in our therapy- and credential-conscious culture. Although professional societies of psychiatrists, psychologists, and social workers keep lists of their members, these directories include only the bare essentials. Counselors who have attended accredited schools, passed their licensure exams, and kept their records clear of any blatantly unprofessional acts are considered therapists in good standing and therefore recommendable. But the lists tell us nothing about a counselor's resources or degree of empathy, both of which are vital concerns in choosing someone who can really help. In addition, many competent counselors in fields that have not yet organized professional societies remain unlisted.

The best and most candid sources of good recommendations are other parents. A local parent group that focuses on the particular problem—a support group for parents of youngsters with substance abuse problems, an alliance for families of emotionally ill children, or a network, such as Tough Love, for those who must stand firm in limiting their children's behavior—can often provide many good referrals. You may also be able to get recommendations from the school guidance counselor or the court system, if your child is involved in it.

Take the time to interview anyone you are considering as a therapist for your child. A brief phone consultation will screen out any obviously poor matches. Then you can interview the remaining candidates in person. As you search, you may be given a lot of advice that runs contrary to your feelings about your child and your parenting. With self-confidence at low ebb, you may feel tempted to follow advice that feels wrong. Keep in mind, however, that your competence as a parent has not evaporated simply because your child is in trouble. You still know your child better than anyone else, however well credentialed he or she may be.

Trust your instincts. Good therapists know that parents are vital to any treatment plan for their children. They see themselves in partnership with parents and as consultants called in to help the whole family. They do not treat the child in a vacuum. Neither do they patronize

Photo by Hildegard Adler

or discount parental impressions of the child.

Having selected a therapist, you can begin the hard work of figuring out the whys of your child's behavior and coming up with some solutions. Both diagnosis and treatment are joint projects. Therapists are not prophets or magicians; they depend heavily on information from the child and the child's family. During the first visit or two, the therapist will probably take a complete physical and emotional history of your child, as well as a detailed family history. (Many emotional and behavioral problems stem from physical or genetic imbalances that respond to medical treatment in conjunction with therapy.) The therapist will probably interview you and your child together and spend time with each of you separately, suggest some psychological testing, and ask permission to contact your child's school as well as any counselor the family has seen over the years. Within three to five visits, you could have a tentative diagnosis.

Your Child in Therapy

Although the details your child shares with the therapist are treated confidentially, you are entitled to helpful feedback. The therapist should be able to sketch the broad outlines of concern, give you a clear overview of the problem, and outline a treatment plan that she or he thinks would be helpful.

Many parents fear that a therapist will blame them for being the source of their child's problem. This fear is well founded: entire systems of therapy have been built on the premise that disturbed children come from disturbed homes. A competent therapist, however, knows that the reverse is also true—that a disturbed child can devastate an otherwise healthy household—and that disturbances can be traced to sources beyond the home. Some children, for example, are greatly troubled by the normal cycle of growth and development; others are affected by hormonal factors. Genetic predispositions can develop into full-blown disturbances, especially during adolescence. Stress can play a role, and peer influence is not be be underestimated. In short, although family dynamics may reinforce a disturbing situation, they need not be the primary cause of the disturbance.

A treatment plan is the therapist's best-educated guess about what combination of therapies would be most likely to help. Recommendations might include individual, group, or family therapy; a self-help group such as Alcoholics Anonymous, Alateen, or Al-Anon; medication;

or short-term care in a structured environment such as a hospital or a residential treatment center. As a rule, therapists treat children on an outpatient basis and try to keep them with their families unless the situation gets completely out of hand.

Because the treatment of emotional disorders is an art and not an exact science, the treatment plan is never set in stone. You can expect a good therapist to fine-tune the plan as you go along. If changes are not forthcoming, if you are not treated respectfully, if you are not considered an active participant in your child's treatment, and if the therapist is not open to discussing these concerns, you probably need to find someone else.

Coping with Family Fallout

When a child is in trouble, the entire family becomes stressed. One sibling may begin to act out, another may decompensate in more dangerous ways, or a parent may face a major crisis in his or her own life. Yet many couples, unable to handle the unbearable admission that the family is no longer functioning well, are reluctant to seek additional help. Parents of children with serious physical illnesses, on the other hand, are quick to recognize stress and ask for help with it. The hesitation to acknowledge the need for family support when a child has a nonphysical problem reflects the societal bias that exists against emotional and mental illness.

Several steps can be taken to stabilize the family. Below are some of them.

Support systems. The key to preventing or reversing family fallout is arranging adequate support for yourself and your spouse. Ideally, family members and friends may be willing to serve as sounding boards and help out in practical ways. If your extended family is geographically or emotionally inaccessible and serious trouble has pared down your list of friends, you will need to cultivate some new supports. A parent group—if one exists locally, or if you can form one quickly—is very helpful. Other parents who have been through similar problems will understand how you feel and will be well equipped to give both support and practical advice without making judgments.

Therapy. In addition to therapy for your troubled child, consider finding a separate therapist for yourself or for the whole family. While interviewing professional helpers, look for someone who is empathic and can listen respectfully. The point is to come away from each session feeling heard and supported, however tough the issues may be. Once you begin therapy, if any of your needs are not being met, it is perfectly all right to voice your concerns or ask your therapist for the support you need.

Family togetherness. It is vital to continue family life even when your child's life is turned upside-down. Keep some perspective, avoid devoting all your resources to the immediate problem, and continue to do things as a family. Everyone needs the family to continue in ways that were satisfying before the crisis arose. The troubled child, especially, needs to see that his or her problems are not powerful enough to tear the family apart—that you as a parent are strong enough to handle the problems (with help), that you will not burn out, and that you can maintain a healthy family life that meets everyone's needs reasonably well.

Family togetherness, as important as it is, ultimately hinges on the severity of the situation. Are the usual family activities only slightly modified, or are they totally disrupted? If one parent can continue working, if brothers and sisters are able to continue their studies, and if everyone is able to pursue at least some individual interests, then the child in trouble is probably best off living at home and taking part in an outpatient treatment or educational program. If, however, family life is seriously compromised by a child who needs too much parental help or supervision—or if the child acts out so dramatically that you can neither go out in public together nor have people in to see you—then it may be best for the child to live away from home, at least temporarily. In deciding whether to provide at-home care or seek the help of a residential treatment program, consider the overall impact on the family of taking full-time responsibility for your troubled child.

Residential treatment. A residential program can meet the needs of the entire family. Treatment usually combines both group and individual therapy with education. The child has access to a therapist 24 hours a day, and the family is asked to participate in the treatment. For the child, such a program can treat the particular problem while providing both a controlled environment and the supports needed to live with other people. For the family, residential treatment can offer a welcome respite after months—or perhaps years—of struggle. With the pressures of full-time responsibility lifted, the family has a chance to recuperate, to learn how to deal with stress, and to explore ways of

Photo by Hildegard Adler

avoiding it. The family also has the opportunity to generate enough collective energy to support and encourage all its members, enough breathing space to be a haven for everyone, and enough laughter to be a place in which people want to be.

To find a good residential treatment program, get referrals from therapists, hospitals, guidance counselors, or parent groups. You can also request a list of programs from your state department of mental health or department of education, or you may search through a guide such as Porter Sargent's *Directory for Exceptional Children*. If the first few programs you contact are full or inappropriate for your child, the people in charge may be able to refer you to other programs that can suit your needs. If you make little progress in your search and the situation becomes urgent, consider the somewhat expensive option of having an educational consultant help you find a program—and some funding for it.

Although residential care is expensive, most families need not pay the whole bill themselves. If treatment is in a hospital, your health insurance company will probably cover most, if not all, of the expenses incurred in the first thirty to sixty days. (Psychiatric hospitalizations are usually fairly short.) If you do not have health insurance, you may be able to get support from the state or from the hospital itself.

More specialized programs—those geared to drug or alcohol abuse—sometimes offer scholarship spaces as well as airfare to the program site. When special programs are recommended, most insurance companies will cover these costs separately from any psychiatric costs. Your local department of education might also agree to share costs with your social services department or the department of mental health.

The Future

Families worry about the future of a child in trouble—and understandably so. A glance at the numbers of adults who continue to abuse drugs and alcohol, who continue to have violent outbursts, and who still have not found themselves long after others their age are well launched can be unnerving. "What if my child never pulls together?" is an often-heard refrain.

Although it is always possible that a child will not outgrow the difficulties, most children in trouble can be helped. Those most likely to get better come from families who acknowledge the problem, insist on getting help for it regardless of the child's resistance, and continue building a home life that supports all family members. There are no guarantees, but we can stack the deck in our children's favor.

Thoughtful parents raise their children for the sheer joy of it. They hope their children will be happy and productive, and they guide them and give them tools to help them grow. Most children respond to that—sooner or later—and develop into the kinds of people who inspire their parents' delight and pride. A few continue to challenge their families and themselves. Whatever the outcome may be, the good experiences that we have shared with our children endure. These are what sustain families through the hardest of times.

For More Information

Brans, Jo, and Margaret Taylor Smith. *Mother, I Have Something to Tell You*. Garden City, N.Y.: Doubleday, 1987.

Curran, Dolores. *Traits of a Healthy Family*. New York: Harper & Row, 1983.

Doyle, Patricia, and David Behrens. *The Child in Crisis*. New York: McGraw-Hill, 1986.

Keals, Yvonne. *The Mother of David S*. New York: St. Martin's Press, 1985.

Miller, Alice. *The Drama of the Gifted Child*. New York: Basic Books, 1981.

Pizzo, Peggy. *Parent to Parent*. Boston: Beacon Press, 1983.

Porter, Sargent. *Directory for Exceptional Children*. (Available from 11 Beacon Street, Boston, MA 02108; 617-523-1670.)

Substance Abuse and Kids: A Directory of Education, Information, Prevention, and Early Intervention Programs. (Available from The Oryx Press, 2214 North Central at Encanto, Phoenix, AZ 85004-1483; 800-457-ORYX.)

17

ROCK CLIMBING

Ross Herbertson

Rock climbing provides an ideal metaphor for approaching apparently insurmountable obstacles. The vivid experience of clinging to a cliff arouses intense emotional reactions—anger, fear, hope, self-doubt, mistrust, exultation. Although the rock remains impartial and unchanging, each climber's reaction registers as uniquely as his or her own fingerprint. Rock climbing offers an unmistakable reading of one's state of being.

Climbing also offers successes that bolster self-esteem. Everyone's safety depends on cooperation and mutual support. As the cheers of the ground crew propel a climber ever higher, everyone shares in the exuberance of accomplishment. The shift from "I can't, I can't" to "I did it!" provides a resource of self-confidence that can be drawn upon in the face of the next challenge a teenager faces.

For more than three years I have led weekly programs for teenagers who are in residential treatment centers for chemical dependency. These young people must admit to behavior that is out of control and frequently judge themselves to be failures. Rock climbing has proven to be a valuable therapeutic tool for these adolescents. The intensity of the experience can shatter dysfunctional defense mechanisms, and knowing that such a positive experience could only happen while sober can inspire a renewed commitment to the struggle for recovery. Because the program fosters success, it often galvanizes both individual and group momentum for healing.

* * *

The teenagers emerge from the van as if all the world were a stage. A girl in tight white shorts and a bulky white sweater gingerly points her toe toward the dirt. She is knocked aside by a boy whose head is half-shaved, half-shaggy. He explodes from the seat behind hers, leaps through the air, and staggers to regain his balance. A triumphant grin

Photo by Sam Forencich

stretches across his face, as if he has completed a difficult maneuver on his skateboard. A boy wearing black leather and chrome imperiously plants his feet in the soil and folds his arms across his chest. A mop of hair hides the face of the next person, who wears an army jacket and torn jeans. I make a mental note to discover if this is a boy or a girl. He/she fumbles for a cigarette, apparently unable to breathe without it. When all ten recovering alcoholics and addicts have made their descent from the van, I ask them to assemble in a circle.

"Each of us will have a different experience rock climbing today," I announce, "even though we'll all climb the same rock." They respond one by one. White Sweater professes to love the outdoors. Skateboarder feigns indifference. Black Leather, arms still folded, admits he is afraid but eager. Army Jacket expresses a confidence that stems from her experience in breaking and entering. Three others direct hostility toward me. Two more shudder like racehorses impatient to start. The last one looks down and says nothing. We pick up the lunches, helmets, harnesses, ropes, and the clanking, colorful rack of climbing hardware and trudge up the knoll.

"You mean this is it? This rock here? This'll be easy," comments one crew member, with several others in accord. Some of the teens swarm around the base of the outcropping as the others begin pawing through the lunch bags and sneaking furtive glances toward the top of the cliff. As they devour their sandwiches, many of the teenagers huddle out of the wind in the sunny lee of some nearby boulders.

I excuse myself from the lunch group and carry the hardware around the rock to set up the protection for climbing. Peering over the edge to the ground thirty-five feet below, I watch the tops of their heads as the teens jostle about. When they seem finished with lunch, I toss down the ends of both climbing ropes, whereupon the group buzzes like disturbed bees in a beehive. When I get back to the bottom, the crew stirs restively. Then we don the helmets and harnesses to the accompaniment of several jokes inspired by the awkwardness of the gear.

Filing around to the side of the rock, we spread out along its base. I specify a three-foot height limit, after which everyone climbs up onto the face. We practice different handholds and footholds and try moving in various postures. For the next exercise, I call out, "Now, we'll climb all the way." Jaws drop in disbelief. "I don't mean climb to the top," I explain. "That's too dangerous! We'll climb the whole rock sideways along the base. That's called traversing."

Staying within two feet of the ground, the group bunches and stretches like a giant inchworm taking the measure of the rock. We repeat the traverse, this time no more than six inches from the ground, which limits our choice of footholds and handholds. The next traverse we perform blindfolded, with a buddy holding onto each harness to *both* regulate the height and act as a spotter. By now, even the most reserved participants move fluidly on the rock, with hands and feet programmed for success.

We clamber back around to the ropes and work on belaying skill-sways to hold the ropes to protect the climber. The teenagers learn that although the rope exists for their protection, in case they lose their grip, it does not assist in the actual climbing. Our belay system involves four people: the climber, who is tied to one end of the rope; the primary belayer, who takes up the slack as the climber moves up the rock; the secondary belayer, who provides double insurance to the climber; and the monitor, who ensures that the other three are focused on the task at hand. As a group of ten we are able to occupy two ropes simultaneously, practicing the various commands and techniques and giving everyone a chance to rotate through all four positions.

At this point, a palpable tension grips the group. Skateboarder stonewalls Army Jacket, who is agitated about something. Others respond to them harshly. Some mill about and physically bounce off each other, generating concerns about everything but climbing. Each individual finds a unique expression for his or her fear. Then we circle again.

"Something's going on here," I voice for the group. "What's eating us?" Skateboarder hisses his frustration at the group's slow pace. He complains that we are taking so long, we might just as well go home now. Army Jacket counters with irritation, noting that Skateboarder's shenanigans are distracting us and slowing down the process. White Sweater moans that she never wanted to come in the first place, that the whole idea is stupid. Black Leather attacks me for interfering with his desire to enjoy himself away from the city. Gradually, like the tapering of a rainstorm, the pressure behind all these feelings begins to ease.

I turn the decision back to them, saying. "Look, this is your day. If you've had enough, we can leave. I've said all along that what you make of the day is up to you. I can't force you to climb if you don't want to. And I certainly won't allow anyone to belay if he or she is unable to focus on safety. I'd like to go for it, but I'll agree to whatever you decide. Let's sit down, go around the circle, and say what you'd like to do from here." Some murmur, some are impassioned, but unanimously they agree that they want to climb. I propose that their focus—on supportiveness and safety consciousness—will be my way of determining their commitment and that if this focus slips, I reserve the right to cancel the rest of the day. They agree to these conditions. Afterward, I review safety points, explain the differences between the two routes up the rock, and give a little pep talk. Then we all hold hands in silence.

After a moment, everyone gets up and moves into position as if choreographed. The arousal of adrenaline, now focused, fuels a sincere support for the two volunteers tying onto the ropes in preparation for climbing.

Army Jacket, running through the verbal commands with her belayers, steps onto the more difficult route. While reaching for a handhold, she loses her footing and jolts all six inches back to the ground. She is visibly shaken, but her feisty aplomb simmers into hot determination. She remounts the rock and, in two quick moves, climbs waist high. Clawing for another handhold, she scrambles and then loses her grip. As she dangles on the end of the rope, her legs wheel cartoonlike, flailing for something to stand on. Her determination flares into anger. She curses the belayers, curses the rock, and curses herself. Then she demands to be lowered to her feet. As she stands on the grass panting, she pounds the rock with her fist. "It looks so easy," she fumes, glancing back at her belayers. They calmly reassure her and jokingly tell her to imagine she is climbing a fire escape in search of an unlocked window. She chuckles and turns to the rock with renewed enthusiasm. Half a dozen elegant moves later, she stands on a ledge eight feet above the ground.

Pausing to catch her breath, she gestures triumphantly to the folks below. Then she turns her attention to Skateboarder who, on the less difficult route, has decided to try his first climb blindfolded. He impatiently scans the rock with wide sweeps of his hands, groping for a hold. Army Jacket shouts words of encouragement to him, whereupon his searching takes on a less desperate pace.

Army Jacket, meanwhile, resumes her climb but is suddenly unable to find any worthwhile footholds or handholds. She bellows in frustration, pressing her forehead against the stone. "What am I supposed to do, fly?" she pleads. I offer her the bleak reassurance that she is right—there is nothing to hold onto—which is why this is the more difficult route. I instruct her to trust her feet and use her hands for balance only. Returning from her despair, she takes two steps up the increasingly slick face, begins to panic, notices that Skateboarder is higher than she is, and sinks back down to the ledge. Although she abuses the belayers, they do not seem to take her anger personally. When she demands to be lowered to the bottom, they counter with a suggestion to try again. Their patience feeds her resolve, and she repeats her previous two moves up the cliff.

Skateboarder, meanwhile, arrives at the top of the rock, finds a secure spot, sits down, and removes his blindfold. Then he grimaces at the brightness of the sunlight and covers his face with his hands. After giving his eyes some time to adjust, he peeks through his fingers at the cheering throng below, raises both fists in salute, and howls. "I never thought I'd be so glad to see! What a killer view!" He sits in reverie for a few moments, observing the dried grasses rippling in the breeze, the golden meadow undulating down to the broad bay below, and the distant peaks rising above the low-lying roads and buildings.

The attention below shifts back to Army Jacket, who now concentrates her efforts with a grim determination. Creeping, grunting, and panting, she claws her way up another step, and then another. The pulsing chants of support from below push her ever higher, until she arrives at a place where she can find neither a sliver of rock to grasp nor a bulge against which to press her toe. The crew shouts in a frenzy of excitement. With this, her body recoils, then springs up, her right hand groping madly until it catches and her left foot swinging higher until it finds a tiny nubbin. She hangs like a spider, sprawled across the rock and gripping ferociously while her lower foot inches up a shallow crack. Her legs bob like a sewing-machine needle as she begins to drag her left hand down the coarse surface of the rock. Finding nothing, she throws her hand back up, and it lands on a flake as thin as a credit card. To her it is a hold, so she releases her other hand to grab a nob the size of two stacked nickels. She is now twenty-five feet up in the air, holding onto virtually nothing and sprawled diagonally across the face of the cliff, her breath coming in shallow grunts.

Everyone on the ground is absorbed in her concentration. Their cheers sustain her. Suddenly, her arm arcs to a ledge, her leg swings up, and she lunges, flopping her torso over a tiny ledge. She swims her legs up until she can crouch on it, sobbing and shaking. As the teens below dance and hoot, Army Jacket collects herself for the remaining ten feet of the climb, which turn out to be easy by comparison. In a matter of moments, she slumps atop the cliff. Her shoulders hunch, her head hangs, yet she manages a weak wave to the throng below. As she watches them jumping about, a smile creeps onto her face. Then she waves the Hawaiian finger sign, meaning "All right!" and disappears from view. In a moment, she emerges from behind a rock and, glad to be back at ground level, falls into a long hug with White Sweater.

One after another, the teenagers encounter their challenges and overcome them with varying degrees of trauma. The next climber fumbles with Army Jacket's rope in his eagerness to follow her. Knowing it is difficult but believing it is possible, he scampers up to the first ledge before getting stumped by the lack of holds. Black Leather, who has already begun climbing, surmounts the less difficult route with few problems. When the rope is thrown down again, one of the girls asks for a blindfold. The coaxing of the group eventually convinces White Sweater to try the less difficult side. She sets off, announcing repeatedly that she cannot do it, until someone points out that she is already higher than our heads—a realization that propels her up the remainder of the cliff.

After everyone has climbed once, we begin a second round. This time, the participants manufacture their own difficulties, trying a harder route or climbing blindfolded. Skateboarder, on his third climb, ascends the more difficult side wearing a blindfold while his ground support stares transfixed by his courage.

Eventually, the focus begins to falter. A monitor points out to one set of belayers that they are joking around rather than watching their climber. Two girls dig out the leftovers from lunch. Army Jacket pleads for a cigarette. So, after the two climbers on the rock have reached the top and returned, we gather into another circle. Although some individuals express the desire to keep climbing, the majority admit that they have lost their drive, and we agree to end the day. White Sweater gathers the helmets onto their sling, Black Leather ties together the harnesses, and I coil the ropes and break down the protection.

Then we gather into a final circle. I ask if anyone objects to my taking notes. No one does, so I pull out paper and pen and record the comments as these tough and troubled teenagers eloquently open their hearts.

Black Leather speaks first: "On the streets, I trust no one. Whenever I work with other people, they never hold up their end. Today was the opposite—I knew I could trust all of you. We worked together doing the exercises. When I climbed, I knew someone was holding the other end of the rope, and I knew I could trust that person. It's such a relief to learn to trust."

Skateboarder explains: "I'm one of those guys with a lot of self-will. I even tried to get out of climbing this morning because of my self-will. At first, I said I didn't want any advice—I wanted to do the hard side my way. But if it weren't for the whole group cheering me on, I never would have made it. If I just let you all in, I know you can really help me. I know that, but I keep forgetting. It sure was clear to me today."

White Sweater talks as if the words were pressurized. "I thought my big issue was trust," she says, "but today I found out it's vulnerability. When I was standing on the rock, I was paralyzed and couldn't let myself do it at first. I got stuck and thought I was going to die. I just wanted to quit and have you lower me down slowly. I was afraid to climb any more, but you know what? I'm here and I did it, and I'm kinda in shock that I did. What I got out of it was trying something new. Now I won't be so afraid to try something hard, because I know I can put my heart into it and do it."

Army Jacket speaks slowly, searching for words. "I got stuck with no footholds or handholds, and then I fell twice," she points out. "And each time I only fell three inches, and so I knew White Sweater was at the other end of the rope, and I trusted her. Thank you, girl, for being there for me. Things didn't work out like I thought, so I stepped back and looked at the whole thing. The rock seemed like the obstacles in my life, and I had to stop and figure out how to deal with the problems rather than just pushing on. The rope seemed like the support I need to meet the challenges in my life. I was afraid. Both my legs were shaking, and I felt like throwing up, and I said, 'I can't do it. I can't, I can't.' But you guys helped me, cheering for me and telling me I could. I feel really grateful. I've had a lot of struggles in my life, and now I'm starting to figure out that each struggle gives me more courage to move on and that when I get through each one I have a sense of accomplishment."

PART III:
PARENTS AND TEENS

Photo by Hildegard Adler

18

THE JOYS AND TRAVAILS OF PARENTING TEENAGE CHILDREN

Bruce Bassoff and Evelyn Silten Bassoff

Sad for You, Funny for Me *(Bruce Bassoff)*

When my daughter Leah was three, she and I used to get up at the same time every morning, and we developed a morning ritual. First I prepared her breakfast of cereal and fruit. Then I made my own breakfast, which, since I was on a health food kick at the time, consisted of a drink made of papaya juice, wheat germ, nutritional yeast, and dates. Since my daughter never stopped chattering from the moment she got up, I divided my attention as best I could between responding to her and attending to our breakfasts. One morning, as I answered one of her queries, I knocked over the container in which I had just blended my drink. As the viscous concoction spread over the kitchen floor and I counted to ten in an effort not to lose my temper, my daughter crowed hilariously.

At that point I decided to teach her a lesson in what the poet Shelley called "the sympathetic imagination." I asked her, "Do you think that's funny?"

"Yes," she replied. "It's very funny."

"I want you to imagine," I said, "that you and Daddy are walking into town to get ice cream cones."

Having a passion for ice cream, my daughter could imagine that easily. She lit up at the thought.

"We go to the ice cream store and I get you a pistachio ice cream and me a coffee one."

Her face lit up even more.

"Now we're walking home and we're licking our ice cream, but sud-

Photo by John Schoenwalter Photography

denly you trip and drop your cone. The ice cream's all ruined. Would that be funny?"

My daughter's eyes filled with tears. "No," she said. "That would be sad."

At this point I figured I had her.

"Now," I said, "Daddy went to all that trouble making his drink. He put in the papaya juice, he put in the wheat germ, he put in the yeast, he put in the dates, and he mixed it all up. Then he dropped it, and it spilled all over the floor. Is that funny or sad?"

"Sad for you, funny for me," she replied.

Far from being frustrated with her for not getting the lesson, I was delighted. As a child I had been precociously empathic and responsible. Both my parents had contracted polio when they were children, and the disease had left them with physical disabilities. As a result, I had been riddled with guilt for being physically whole. My three-year-old daughter's repudiation of my unreasonable expectations of empathy and responsibility delighted me. It also confirmed a feeling I had had from the moment she was born: complete confidence in her.

For reasons that are still not completely clear to me, I have always projected onto Leah my strong, adventurous side. I realize, of course, that part of the reason Leah, now nineteen, *is* so adventurous and self-confident is the fact that I encouraged those traits; but I always felt sure—even when she was little—that she could negotiate successfully any normal challenges. Though Leah experienced some trouble as she grew up—in nursery school, for example, she became afraid of one of her teachers who, she believed, was going to take her away from us—by and large she managed transitions quite well. In fact, she looked forward to them, whereas I had had difficulty with them while I was growing up.

I delighted in sharing my imagination with Leah. When she was little, she and I used to go for walks, and I created voices for flowers and berries and made them talk to her. I told her stories and imitated the voices of *Sesame Street* characters as I put her to sleep, cut her nails, or just sat with her on a rainy day. I enjoyed her own imaginative endeavors and was an appreciative audience when she put on plays, drew, or made little things for imaginary friends. More than that, however, I enjoyed the ways in which she, even as a young girl, surpassed my own efforts and experience. I had always had trouble with my hands—fixing things, arts and crafts, school projects. My daughter, however, like my wife, has always been extremely competent in drawing, painting, cutting, pasting, and the like. I experienced through her the vicarious satisfaction of completing projects I either botched or failed to do in school.

As my daughter became a teenager, it was interesting, amusing, and painful—and sometimes all those at once—to see the ways in which she separated from me and my wife. For one thing, she went through a stage in which everything my wife and I did embarrassed her. She was constantly "mortified" by the way we looked, sounded, and acted. In fact, one weekend when two other couples and we shared a cabin in Estes Park—each couple having two children the same age as our children—we kept a "mortification" chart to see which parents mortified their kids most in the course of the weekend. One Halloween in particular, I embarrassed Leah extremely by singing sixties songs with a friend as we all walked down to the Boulder Mall to participate in the "mall crawl" of costumed people.

She also repudiated, with great determination, what she considered my wife's and my overconcern with health and with the body. Though I tended to worry about Leah much less than my wife did, I did worry about health in general. My daughter seemed to flaunt her taste for food that had sugar and artificial preservatives and her *dis*taste for food that we regarded as better for her. When she gave me her list of things to buy at the supermarket, she made sure to specify items like "normal" bread or "normal" peanut butter to make sure I did not buy the health food variety. She also refused to exercise and to get as much sleep as we wanted her to. In defending herself against our concern, she pointed to the fact that she was the healthiest member of the family. For example, she said, she never missed school.

Most painful for me—but also most important for me—she repudiated my weaknesses. Though Leah is a very sweet and outgoing person, she can be cold when she needs to be. Though she enjoys my humor and my creativity, she has no patience whatsoever with the fear or depression I sometimes display. Though I've sometimes wanted her sympathy when I've gone through a particularly bad time, I've been grateful to her for withholding it and for insisting that I be a strong father.

My perception is that Leah's adolescence was close to ideal. The most important influence on her at that time, besides her parents, was a young people's acting company called the Boulder Act. From the time she was nine, she participated in acting classes. These classes encouraged her to get in touch with her feelings and to find efficient and eloquent ways to express them. They provided her and other kids with a safe environment in which to think about, talk about, and act out experiences that would otherwise have been problematic, even dangerous. As she shared these experiences year after year with some of the same kids, she formed a strong bond with them. When she became a member of the acting company and thus eligible to participate in full theatrical productions, she was encouraged to take risks that I would have found completely daunting at a similar age. I still remember her doing a piece from *Cat on a Hot Tin Roof* in which, at a relatively undeveloped fourteen, she had to play a sexy Maggie the Cat.

The discipline and commitment that the "Act" fostered, and Leah's strong sense of identity within a group of like-minded friends, made her adolescence a snap. Whatever quarrels my wife and I had with her, they were small and short-lived, usually involving reminders on her part that she was strong and healthy and did not need our solicitude.

If bringing up my daughter has by and large been easy, bringing up my son has been much more demanding. My feelings toward him, moreover, have been much more ambivalent.

It's possible that I feel even closer to my son than I do to my daughter. From the beginning, Jonathan was more physically aggressive than Leah, and I enjoyed rolling around and wrestling with him. As he got older, we would tussle and romp in ways that made the women in the house complain. "Go outside if you're going to roughhouse!" they would chorus. Sometimes Leah would begin to sing "The sun will come out to-mor-row," a song that both Jonathan and I hate, and that would make us stop.

I shared my athletic prowess with my son from an early age—something that my father could never do with me. I taught him to throw on the front lawn, and I taught him to catch by throwing high flies that he learned to track and to hold onto. I taught him everything I knew about baseball and basketball, and when he began participating in organized sports, I went to all his games. In addition, the two of us were active spectators, frequently attending baseball and basketball games, and each morning we shared the sports news. Having grown up in a house where it seemed that my father was sometimes excluded, or excluded himself, from my sister's and my upbringing, I relished the fact that my son gravitated toward me more than he

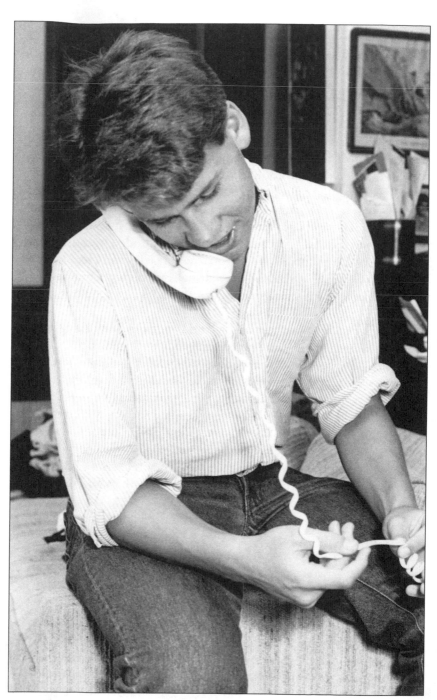

Photo by Hildegard Adler

did toward my wife. He was my "main man," and I was his.

Yet, precisely because of our closeness, I came to fear that some genetic tape would cause my son to experience the same fears, weaknesses, and pains I had experienced while growing up. I worried about Jonathan much more than I did about Leah, and he, in turn, seemed almost preternaturally sensitive to my moods. If, when he was little, I got angry at him, he acted as if the world were coming to an end, and I felt like a brute. Though I loved him intensely and enjoyed his company, I did not have the same fundamental faith in his strength and resiliency as I did in my daughter's.

Jonathan was aware of these projections, but they were just some of the problems he had to deal with in adolescence. His parents were both successful, high-powered people who had achieved a degree of public recognition. His sister had always loved school and was an honors student at Boulder High. She had enjoyed success and public visibility in both the Boulder Act and in her high school's drama program. In her senior year, she appeared in a play that I wrote and got good reviews in all the major papers. She also played Juliet in a high school production and was accepted by a first-rate private college. My son felt as if he were living in our collective shadows. He never derived much satisfaction from school, which stimulated him little and stretched his abilities even less. He got most of his self-esteem from sports, but as he got older, he found it more difficult to excel.

Throughout adolescence, Jonathan has been moodier and more given to depression than Leah. But he has also, perhaps, gained greater depth. Perhaps because of his interest in sports, but also perhaps because of his sense of himself as an underdog in our family, he has come to identify with minority groups and becomes indignant at stereotyping and discrimination. As his father, I feel that he has contributed more to my own growth process than my daughter has. As I've worked in psychotherapy to accept my own strengths, I've become better able to cope with the ways in which he tests me and to insist that he be strong also. I've gradually become less guilty when I feel angry toward him, and he has become firmer and more confident in standing up to me. Whereas earlier he was overly empathic, now he, too, can say, "Sad for you, funny for me."

As I've encouraged him to develop his strengths, so he has encouraged me. For example, for years people in my household avoided me whenever I made it known that I was going to try to fix something.

Through much trial and error, I've recently become more adept at mechanical tasks, and Jonathan has often helped me or kept me company while I've struggled through them.

I was once asked, in the sixth grade, to put together a model airplane. Having no confidence in my ability to do such things, I balked at the idea and told my mother how uncomfortable I was at the prospect of doing it. My mother went to school and asked the teacher to excuse me from what she considered a task unworthy of my great intelligence. "I wish," I said to Jonathan when I told him this story, "that someone had made me do it, that someone had convinced me it didn't matter whether it turned out great or awful as long as I tried." Recently, Jonathan bought me a model airplane kit and told me that we would assemble it together. In a sense, that model airplane is a metaphor for our whole relationship. These days, I often have the experience of swift and secure flight.

Don't Worry *(Evelyn Silten Bassoff)*

The day after I brought my newborn home from the hospital, I discovered a little bump on her head. Because I am an expert worrier, I became anxious that her skull was somehow deformed. Although our pediatrician struck me as a kind and gentle man, I hesitated contacting him. Would he type me as a hysterical, overreactive new mother who made mountains out of molehills? Much worse, would he confirm my terrible fear? When, after a few days, my worry did not pass, I finally mustered the courage to telephone him.

"Doctor Rapaport," I stumbled, "I'm really sorry to disturb you with what is no doubt a silly worry."

"Mrs. Bassoff," he broke in, "between 8:00 a.m. and 9:00 a.m.—and it is now exactly 8:32—I attend only to new mothers' silly worries. You have no reason to be apologetic about calling me, and I am happy to help you if I can."

The kind doctor then assured me that baby Leah's bump was innocuous and that I had no reason to be concerned about it. In the months that followed, I found it easier to telephone Dr. Rapaport during "silly worry hour." Inevitably, he provided the reassurances I craved. "Don't worry, Mrs. Bassoff, you and Leah are doing just fine," he would say. But, alas, Leah got older, graduated from her baby doctor's care, and I was forced to relinquish Dr. Rapaport's wise counsel. However, my silly worries about Leah did not melt away.

During Leah's early adolescence, as she necessarily liberated herself from my protective care and control, I tended to fret and worry over her even more than I had when she was younger. Was she eating enough? Was she getting enough sleep? Or enough fresh air? Or enough exercise? Was she secure among her friends? Was she really happy? Leah rarely complained about her life; my husband was absolutely confident that she was a well-adjusted, healthy girl; her teachers raved about her. But I worried and worried. Although Leah certainly provided me with much lightness and joy, more than anyone else in my life, she stirred my anxiety. But why?

One day as I was staring at Leah's face—a habit of mine that annoyed her terribly—I had a vision. Gazing into her soft hazel eyes, I saw an image of myself as a young girl. There it was, shockingly clear: my own sad adolescent face shining from my daughter's sparkling eyes. Months later, with the help of a psychotherapist, I began to understand how this strange vision was connected to my anxiety regarding Leah.

As a young teenager, I was rather sickly—underweight, underdeveloped, and poorly coordinated. Comparing myself to my more robust girlfriends, I had felt frail and unprepared for life's challenges. Because Leah and I are physically alike and because we have been so close, I had sometimes merged our personalities. My overconcern for Leah was, at least in part, a displaced solicitude for the vulnerable teenager I once was. For me, learning to be a good mother to my teenage daughter required separating my phantom or inner child from her. I am not Leah; Leah is not me. We are different women.

Although differentiating myself from my daughter was (and is) a difficult task for me, I am not similarly burdened with struggles of separation with my teenage son. Jonathan, it seems, has always insisted on a certain distance between us. When he could not adequately protect himself from my hovering/smothering mothering, my husband came to his aid, and together they held me at bay.

As an infant, Leah was blissfully content nursing in my arms. Jonathan, on the contrary, seemed more interested in the goings-on around him than in the breast and, consequently, pulled and yanked away from me. Unlike Leah, who enjoyed being taken on long walks in her carriage or Snugli, Jonathan hated being constrained in his umbrella stroller. Indeed, by stiffening his body and thrusting it for-

Photo by John Schoenwalter Photography

ward, he often managed to toddle away from me with the stroller strapped to his back, so that he appeared half human baby/half turtle. As if this was not enough, after Jonathan mastered unstrapping himself, he discovered the fun of running off with his stroller and ramming it into walls and people. On one excursion to the Museum of Natural History, I remember taking sweet little Leah's hand and guiding her toward the dioramas of dinosaurs, all the while pretending that the pint-sized wildman with the stroller who was terrorizing the museum's visitors did not belong to our family!

By all objective accounts, Jonathan is our more difficult child. While nineteen-year-old Leah has always adjusted easily to the world, Jonathan, at sixteen, still rams against it. Yet, unlike his sister, he does not generally stir my anxiety. When Jonathan shares his frustrations, hurts, and worries with me, I tend not to become overwhelmed by them. Rather than being pulled into sharing in his anxiety, I am able to maintain a certain distance from it, which better allows me to help him through it. Gazing into Jonathan's soft dark eyes, I have never seen myself reflected. I see only a fine, handsome, intelligent, sensitive young man who tries—sometimes gracefully, sometimes awkwardly—to cope with the world.

Somewhere along the way, I learned that being a good parent does not involve sheltering one's children from all of life's hardness and disappointments but rather enabling them to be strong and competent. I also learned that in order to prepare my children to confront life's challenges, I myself must be strong and able. When I turned sixteen, I tried and failed to learn to drive. At age twenty-six, out of dire necessity, I did learn to drive a car with an automatic transmission, but believing myself to be uncoordinated, I was afraid to attempt a manual transmission. Now, at forty-five, I am picking up where I left off as a young woman. With my daughter, who has just driven cross-country, at my side, I am trying to master the shift and clutch. I tend to stall, roll back, or bump along, but Leah encourages me to push on. "Don't worry, Mom," she says cheerfully, "you're doing just fine."

19

SIX WAYS *NOT* TO EMBARRASS YOUR TEENAGER

Penny Colman

Remembering how her parents embarrassed her "all the time" when she was a teenager, Linda Hickson Bilsky, Professor of Education at Teachers College, Columbia University, tries hard not to embarrass her fourteen-year-old daughter Dana. "But I'm not always successful," Bilsky says with a sigh. Dana agrees, "Usually my mother is pretty good about not embarrassing me. But then she'll do something that makes me want to disappear."

Linda Bilsky isn't alone. Most parents acknowledge that they probably embarrass their children despite their efforts not to, an admission that their teenagers, like Dana, confirm. My own three sons, until recently teenagers themselves, are no exceptions. When I asked them if I had ever embarrassed them, my son Stephen said after a tactful pause, "Well, I finally decided it would be more productive if I tried harder to get over being embarrassed."

So, it's inevitable. Although some parents are more embarrassing than others and some teenagers more sensitive than others, at some point all parents are going to embarrass their adolescent offspring. What then can well-meaning parents do to minimize the extent of the damage?

Teenagers I've talked with want their parents to concentrate on *not* doing the *really* embarrassing things—the things that are guaranteed to make even thick-skinned, confident teenagers wince and blush. The following parental practices are most often mentioned by teenagers as examples of what not to do.

1. Don't brag about your teenagers in public. This parental habit topped my children's list of complaints, as it did most teenagers'. This especially holds true when your teenagers are present. Mary Olowin, M.D., a staff psychiatrist at the University of California at Berkeley,

Photo by John Schoenwalter Photography

was surprised to discover that her sons Aaron and Fred were embarrassed "even when what I say is something nice about them." In fact, according to most teenagers, the nicer the parent's comments are, the more embarrassed the teenager feels.

"From the kid's point of view, bragging makes a kid look arrogant," my son Stephen explains. Dana agrees and adds, "I never know what to do. Should I just stand there and look humble or say, 'and don't forget to mention that I also swam the English Channel with my hands tied behind my back?'"

In my experience, parents don't brag to embarrass their teenager; they brag to build his or her self-esteem. At least that's what I have always told myself. However, on reflection I must confess that, in fact, sometimes it hasn't been just my child's self-esteem at stake—it's been my own.

That's not to say that parents should never brag. They just shouldn't do it when their teenagers are around. This is especially true when parents suspect that their bragging has more to do with their own self-esteem than with their teenager's—a motive that teenagers immediately sense and rightfully resist.

2. Don't criticize your teenagers in public. This point seems so obvious that I was astonished it was a problem for so many teenagers. But all too many parents seem to suspend good manners and common sense when it comes to criticizing their teenagers.

"You're so inconsiderate and selfish!" a father shouts at his sixteen-year-old daughter when she comes home late for a dinner party. Another father yells at his fifteen-year-old daughter in front of her friends. "Over little stuff like whether I finished cleaning my room to his satisfaction," says the teenager, who wants to remain anonymous. "I feel so powerless with my friends there because I know if I try to defend myself he'll yell even more." Reg Bannerman, another teenager, says his mother sets him up to be embarrassed in front of his father. "She waits until we're all together and then she starts to make a big deal out of everything—my hair, my clothes, my friends, my music—and makes me look like such a jerk in front of him."

Unfortunately, many parents are unaware of just how much they criticize and pick at their teenagers at family gatherings and in other public situations with complaints ranging from little things like "stand up straight" to big things like "you're never going to amount to anything." It's not that teenagers think their parents shouldn't criticize them; it's that they think their parents should do it in helpful, con-structive ways *and* in private.

3. Don't fight or argue with other adults in public. When I was a child, my father could be counted on to make a scene in a restaurant. He'd argue about the food, the service, anything, as my brothers and I made frequent and prolonged trips to the bathrooms. Unfortunately, several teenagers I talked with had similar stories about parents who terrorize restaurant workers.

Perhaps because I am my father's daughter, as an adult I developed the habit of frequently fuming and fussing in long, slow-moving check-out lines. One day, my son David, who was thirteen at the time, decided he had suffered enough embarrassment. "Mom," he said in a quiet voice as I began to vocalize my frustrations, "if you lose your temper, I'm going to leave and wait for you in the car." I calmed down, perhaps because at some level I remembered my humiliation when my father had acted that way, and focused on talking with David instead of on how fast the line moved.

Shopping malls are also public places where parents embarrass their teenagers. David Skurnick, now a student at Princeton University, remembers his parents arguing in loud voices "about how long to stay, where to shop, and what to buy." Skurnick handled his embarrassment by "walking as far away from my parents as possible without getting lost and hoping that nobody knew I was with them."

An important exception to this "don't" is when parents take stands on matters of conscience and justice such as protesting sexual and racial inequality, providing decent public schools, protecting the environment, and fighting corruption. While initially teenagers may be embarrassed by parents who argue at school board or city council meetings or who write letters to the newspapers, their pride in having parents with principles they'll fight for will ultimately overcome any embarrassment they might feel.

4. Don't be ostentatious. "My dad laughs funny. My mom acts dorky," says Stacy DeVries, eleven, from Winslow, Arizona. Joy Cobbs, eighteen, from Chicago, also finds her parents' behavior embarrassing. "My mother talks all the time, and my father thinks he's a comedian."

This is not to say parents shouldn't be themselves. They should, but with the awareness that in certain situations seemingly innocent parental behavior may embarrass their teenagers. For example, when

I'm cooking and listening to music, I've been known to spontaneously grab whomever walks through the kitchen for a quick dance or to break into my own goofy solo. This is behavior that amuses my kids *except* when their friends are around; then it embarrasses them.

"Take the time to find out what is embarrassing at that time or in that culture," advises Stella Chess, M.D., an eminent child psychiatrist, author, mother of four children, and grandmother of six. When Chess's children were teenagers, the norm was conformity in everything—dress, speech, behavior, attitudes. Now that her grandchildren are teenagers, the norm is individuality. "Parents who understand and appreciate what matters to their teenagers will be less likely to embarrass them," says Chess.

5. Don't forget to screen the photographs you show or the stories you tell. My mother can still embarrass me by telling certain stories from my childhood, stories that she thinks are "cute," and I think are, at best, dumb and, at worst, humiliating. Stella Chess urges parents to "be very sensitive to the stories and mementos you reveal about your teenager's past."

Linda Bilsky makes a point to ask Dana what stories are okay to repeat. "Sometimes I forget, so Dana cues me and I stop."

That's a good system, says Chess. "Parents are people, too, as are teenagers," she points out. "And as long as both parents and teenagers work toward respecting each other's needs and sensitivities, they can overcome even the greatest embarrassment."

6. Don't forget your teenagers are trying to grow up, not down. Of these six ways not to embarrass your teenagers, this is the one I mull over the most. Are my words and behavior going to support and encourage my teenager's independence and self-confidence, or are they going to undermine them? Am I going to make my teenager feel like an infant or like an emerging adult?

"My father still tries to hold my hand when we're crossing a busy street together," says Dana Bilsky with frustration. "It makes me feel like a little girl all over again." Dana's father knows it embarrasses her and he tries to stop himself, but sometimes his protective instincts get the best of him and he finds himself reaching for Dana's hand. Every parent knows the feeling.

Sometimes it's harder to let teenagers grow up than it is younger children because the stakes are higher. The consequences of learning to tie your shoes or to read are very different from the consequences of learning how to drive.

But here is the crux of the parenting experience—being there when you're needed, out of the way when you're not, and able to recognize the difference. It's tough, I know. But we do more than embarrass our children when we don't strive to achieve this; we undermine their self-confidence and inhibit their competence.

20

THE TWENTY-FIVE-YEAR
COMMITMENT

Geeta Dardick

Last night I received a collect call from my son Josh. He goes to junior college in Santa Cruz, California, and it's his first year away from home. "Mom, want to hear the talk on AIDS that I'll be presenting for my final exam?" he asked. "I need your opinion on how it sounds. I want an A in Speech."

I could have answered, "C'mon Josh...you're 19...you're independent...I don't need to worry about your schoolwork anymore, especially on my long-distance phone bill."

Instead, I answered, "Yes, let's hear it...make the beginning stronger...those facts are fascinating...the ending is great...you're speaking a little fast." I gave the needed advice, the strokes of support— to a young man, my son, striving toward adulthood.

When I had my babies in the sixties, I didn't realize that I would still be parenting in the late eighties. I thought my mother role would end when my children reached sixteen, at which point they would get their drivers' licenses and speed away toward total independence. I was wrong.

As children grow older, they will need parental guidance. Between the ages of sixteen and twenty-five, they make numerous important decisions. With your help, they will solve their problems on their own. I'm talking about big issues, such as sex, drugs, alcohol, the military, college, jobs, marriage, money. If you believe in concerned parenting, you will have your hands full during your children's late teens and early twenties.

Please discuss sexuality with your older teens. You'll need to cover every aspect of sex, the pleasures and the risks. In my home, no sexual topic remains taboo. The subject is too important to ignore.

Very few teens ask their parents about sex. Therefore, you should

Photo by Michael Weisbrot

not wait to be asked, or you might wait forever. Instead, talk sex. While driving to the supermarket or doing dishes together, tell them about birth control and venereal disease and, yes, orgasms. Carry on a monologue if you must, but tell them. Even if they do not seem to be listening, they will hear it all.

Most teenage pregnancies occur in families where talk of sex is taboo. Uptight parents cloak sexuality in mystery, tempting the curious child to experience the "secret," just to check it out. A more intelligent approach is to discuss birth control with your children well before they will need the information.

Homosexuality is another issue you'll want to tackle head on. Statistics tell us that one in ten children will grow up to be homosexual. If you and your children have an accepting attitude, it will be much easier for all of you if someone in your family is homosexual. If you are unfamiliar or uncomfortable with the topic, educate yourself about gay rights and develop a liberated attitude that you can share with those close to you.

Support an equally open approach to drugs and alcohol. Why turn these areas into forbidden fruit? I don't tell my older teens to "go get loaded," nor do I say, "You'll be grounded for three months if I ever catch you drinking." I'm a parent, not a policewoman. I refuse to let society's fixation on stimulants interfere with my relationship with my children. I tell them about the dangers of excessive alcohol and drug use, but I still allow them the freedom to party in front of me if they desire. I want them to share their real lives with me, not a cleaned-up version.

Parents should also keep in touch with current styles—fads, music, lingo, clothes—the gestalt of teenness. As young mothers and fathers, it is easy to fall out of touch. We are so busy raising our babies that we forget time is passing quickly. Every decade produces a new society, with new habits and new patterns. How can you provide sympathetic support for your children if you do not understand what is going on in their world?

My husband and I cured our "generation gaposis" by taking the children to rock-and-roll shows. We would buy five tickets, and the entire family would drive four hours down from the hills to Oakland Coliseum. Plunging into the crowd to hear the tunes my teens adored blasting from the ear-shattering amplifiers, I became one with The Who, The Clash, The Scorpions, Loverboy, Tom Petty, REO Speedwagon, and more, more, more. So what if Sam and I were the only folks over forty, pressed together in a sweating sea of 80,000 children in psychedelic T-shirts? What a wonderful education we received for our money.

By the time your children are teens, their cultural milieu may have expanded far beyond today's raucous rock-and-roll concerts. Whatever the expressive medium of their era is, study it, experience it, do it—with them. You will open doors of communication that will benefit all of you.

By letting teenage interests become part of my family's conversational life, I opened myself for an in-depth, long-lasting relationship with my young adult children. Because they find me trustworthy and modern, they let me offer guidance on other important decisions such as education and career. I like having input where it really counts.

Not all of you will have children who want to go on to college after high school. Your son or daughter might prefer to get a job, join the military, travel the world, go to Hollywood, raise veggies in the country, or meditate in an ashram. Whatever your child's decision may be, you can give meaningful counsel.

Should your child choose to pursue an education, you will want to inform yourself about college opportunities so that you can help him or her make wise choices. Coach your son or daughter for the college board exams. High test scores can make a difference. Tour some of the colleges together; it will be a memorable experience for both of you.

Learning on their own works well for some teens, some of the time; however, too much freedom, too soon, can prove disastrous. You would not want to send your teens out on the highway without driving lessons and neither should you send them out into the real world without a plentiful scoop of parental guidance.

In areas of major importance, it is best for parents to practice what has been called "interdependence." If your teens haven't the slightest idea how to choose a college or fill out applications, help them. If they are trying to write their first job resume and don't know the proper format, teach it to them. If they are having an unnecessary clash with their boss, discuss ways to get along with people in authority. If they are buying their first used car, teach them the art of haggling. Develop a partnership; work together. After all, chances are you have been through many of these experiences before. Why expect wonders from your children during round one?

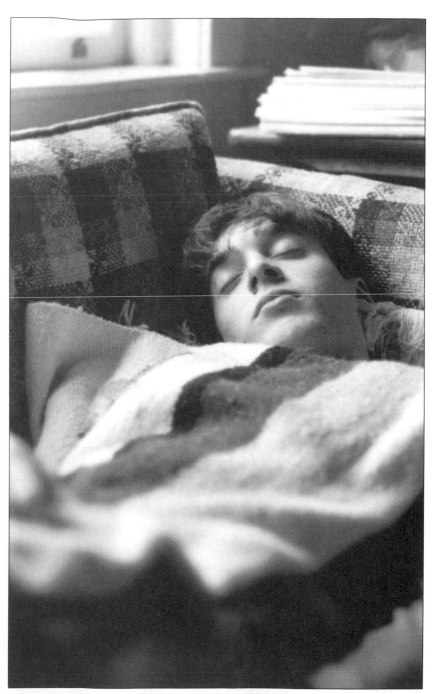

Photo by Marilyn Nolt

We all know that failure can be a learning experience. However, certain types of failures are not worth going through. Too many jobs lost, courses flunked, scholarships missed, boot camps blown, and dollars wasted can add up to a sense of disappointment with life. If you can help your children to develop a positive mental attitude, they will avoid the stresses that plague so many teens and adults today. Watch your language—the messages you send. Give your teens encouragement and tell them how beautiful, smart, and successful they are.

Growing up entails too many new decisions and responsibilities for any teen to handle alone. You will not want to suffocate them and make decisions for them; but neither will you want to cut them loose too soon, so that they founder and fail to reach their own highest goals.

Our children, Caleb, Josh, and Samantha, talk to Sam and me and share with us because we set up a pattern of sharing many years ago. We kept every door open through the terrible twos, the really terrible twelves, the inevitable squabbles, the winter when it rained three weeks straight, the summer when everyone had poison oak, the first dates, the first drinks, the first dramas.

Our children have moved beyond sweet sixteen, but the sharing has not stopped. Instead, the parent-child relationship has improved. I am wiser; they are more mature. I do not try to create my children in my own image, but I try to move them toward their own best image for themselves. And although I expect them to be financially responsible, I also help them with monetary matters when I can.

In our family, I have discovered that parenting is a twenty-five-year commitment. I never suspected that it would last quite this long, but I am thrilled to stay active. Children do not become adults overnight. The change is a long, slow process in which we parents play a meaningful part.

21

ART AND TEENAGERS

Joan Logghe

Raising teenagers has its own surrealism.
Inside a woman's body in designer jeans
is the baby you rocked, an automobile
shifting from first gear to moonscape.
She soars, her arms cocked like Burmese dance.
Clocks melt at curfew hour, torsos disconnect.
As if in dream, she enters the house.

The truth is no longer certain, she says,
"Teenagers have to lie to parents";
it's trompe l'oeil. Midnight drives by
down Route 66, the sixties revisited
by flower children's children. And drugs,
the specter in psychedelic posters
lit by black light.

In conversation, we are cubist and minimalist,
what is square and what is unsaid.
I could be a better mother, I think,
but that's romanticism, rich in pigment
but dated. Too thick,
I slather on coats of oily love,
while talking to teens is high cool.

By now it's pop art comics, op art mazes.
You know they know you don't understand,
ought to try a new form, something Japanese,
three strokes, less said.

You hand her a dishtowel, allowance,
you glance at her laundry once.

But then it softens, you drop the technique.
There's the person you are, flawed
and perfectly human, standing
on your own piece of vinyl flooring,
no wax, low gloss, and the person she is,
ancient art; two women facing the same direction,
Egyptian water urn, Etruscan temple wall,
a bolt of fabric.

Photo by Lisa Law Productions

22

TO MY SON

Daryl Allen

Yesterday was your fifteenth birthday.
You, whom I knew before anyone in the world laid eyes on you.

I wanted to avoid this pain.
I've done careful planning
not to get caught unprepared
like my mother.
Years ago a hometown friend wrote me
she dropped in to visit my mother and found her
crying at the kitchen table,
accepting her prize for raising such strong,
independent kids.
They had, indeed,
grown and gone.
And where did that leave her?
So I have lived differently.
I have my own friends, career, a bed of my own.

Why my sadness?
Because you don't call me from your bath
to bring you a towel, rinse out the shampoo.
I know how to do it without getting it in your eyes.
No chance to read bedtime stories of big trucks and
dinosaurs
mixed with the smell of soap-touched skin
and damp, sweet hair.

Photo by Michael Weisbrot

And even though the last thing I wanted to do on a cold
Saturday morning was drive you to your soccer game,
I miss sitting with the other moms and dads
with whom the only thing I have in common
are the green-jerseyed boys in too-big shorts
chasing across the wet grass.

I knew you were growing up,
but I wasn't ready when the Star Wars posters
changed to Charlie's Angels with nipples showing.
I should have known when Wonder Woman went up.
She was too sexy to be a super-hero.

I'm not used to your deep voice,
your towering over me,
your glossy of Mick Jagger in leather pants stretched
over skinny hips.
I'm not used to your hard edge.

I've read the chapter on adolescence in my child
development book,
and although I understand your choosing values
different from mine,
I don't have to like it.
To be honest, I prefer my chubby preschooler
who liked doing things with me,
who thought our world was *the* world.

Isn't this too early?

We didn't have stashes and paraphernalia
at age fourteen,
and pass a joint in somebody's car at ten o'clock break
in classes at school.
My book about passages says,
if not earlier, then later.
But who holds my hand
while you try it out now?

If I had a choice
I'd probably opt for the four-year-old I picked up from
day care, put on the merry-go-round, and waved to
every time his horse came around.
I don't know the rules for Boardwalk,
New Wave,
jam sessions in the garage.
I guess we'll get through it
as we did the guns and green-army-men stage
and the after-school clashes with the street kids.

Probably this breach between us will narrow
after it gets wide enough
for you to try out being you,
and I get used to it.

Right now,
I'm missing my little friend.

23

TRUST, RESPONSIBILITY, AND LETTING GO

Kathleen G. Auerbach

As the parent of a teenager, I am bombarded—sometimes almost daily—by messages in the print and visual media about the difficulty of this period. And in spite of a generally enjoyable parenting experience, our family has had its share of stresses. Two recent events have sensitized me to two related issues—use of the family car and teenage sexuality—that involve adolescents. The first incident involved my son, who lived through the totaling of our only car with minor physical injuries. The second involved a friend's daughter and her first experience with sexual intimacy.

In both cases, trust was the key issue. In the first instance, I had to come to terms with my own fears about "the other driver" and whether I was comfortable allowing my child to demonstrate to me that he could drive without being threatened. *He* was confident of his ability to drive safely; *I* was the one who had to learn to trust again. Our first driving sessions after the accident were, at my insistence, limited to residential streets with little traffic and next to no forward velocity. He accused me of acting like he was learning to drive all over again! Eventually we progressed to city traffic but still avoided the toll roads and superhighways reminiscent of the accident site. Only after a month of tentative experimentation was I able to comfortably turn the car over to him without biting my lower lip and whitening my knuckles in fear of anticipated consequences I could neither prevent nor control.

With the giving of such trust, I again expect him to be responsible—for himself and any other person in the car. I expect that his actions will support my trust in his skills as a good driver and in the blessedly quick reflexes of youth. Thus, we can each face the future feeling reasonably good about tomorrow. One result of our experience is that

Photo by Michael Weisbrot

I now face only two (minor by comparison) issues relating to the car and a teenage driver: a high insurance premium and a perpetually empty gas tank (even though I drive fewer miles and our new car has a larger fuel tank).

The second incident, involving sexual expression, echoes through my mind every time I see a teenage mother on the postpartum floor housing the hospital lactation clinic and my office. Will my dear friend's daughter avoid pregnancy and the many sexually transmitted diseases it is possible to contract? Is she taking positive steps that result from conscious action to avoid these pitfalls, or is she taking the "ostrich approach" of ignoring problems in the hope that they will go away? Clearly, an unplanned pregnancy can yield a consequence considerably more serious and of potentially longer term than that of an auto accident. That teens do not always recognize this fact is but one facet of the problem that such a pregnancy represents.

In thinking about these issues as they relate to this young woman, whom I remember vividly as a girl not yet rounded by puberty, I consider some questions that all young men and women should ask themselves, questions I would like to ask my friend's daughter.

Are you going to have privacy? In my day, the privacy for sexual experimentation and discovery was often available only in the back seat of a car. Although this was considered romantic in the movies, in reality it required the flexibility of a contortionist. The alternative was a motel room, and none of my friends would consider such a site. Today, privacy can be had easily if either child has the key to an empty house: his or her own. How many working parents' beds have served as the initiation site for the blooming sexuality of their sons or daughters?

This new privacy provides the opportunity to more carefully consider options and their related risks. Can the teen be assured that a parent will not come home early or unexpectedly; that a sibling will not appear; or that a neighbor will not investigate to determine why people are home when they usually are not? Talking about the merits of privacy and where it can be obtained may result in a decision to wait rather than in one to hurriedly consummate a relationship. Making love is an experience that is truly enhanced only when it can be savored.

Who is responsible for not having a baby? It is not sufficient for one party to think that the other party will do this. If neither one assumes the responsibility, each may have to face consequences far more

serious—for more people—than the difficulty of considering the question. To answer the question requires a degree of communication that
seems appropriate to encourage. Such communication can lessen the
likelihood of impulsive behavior.

*Has each of the partners determined that neither will feel bad tomorrow
about what occurred today?* This also requires communication. If either
of the partners, upon reflection, is unconvinced that he or she will
feel good later about what they are contemplating today, perhaps
both need to reconsider why they are engaging in the behavior. While
sex partners may not always look one another in the eye after the act,
no one can escape looking at himself or herself the next day. How
many parents have asked their teenagers to face themselves and consider how they feel *about themselves* after a particular action? This may
be the single most appropriate deterrent to impulsive behavior, far
more effective than all the groundings and physical punishments that
so often result in resentment and further rebellion.

Where is my friend, the mother of this young woman who has chosen not to wait until marriage to experience the intensity of sexual
expression? She has decided to trust her daughter and her daughter's
partner to act responsibly. I am attempting to do the same each time
my son gets behind the wheel of our car.

Consider whose is the greater task: the teenager's to act responsibly
or the parent's to trust. Perhaps because I am a parent, my vote falls
on the trust side of the equation. Trusting requires that the loving parent refrain from making judgmental statements or acting out of fear,
anger, or myriad other emotions. To trust is to care by standing aside
and offering the freedom to be responsible. This freedom says, more
plainly than any number of words, that the youngster is being given
the opportunity to engage in responsible adult behavior. Surely that is
what most teens strive to achieve.

Lately I have become aware of the ways in which many young
animals assume adult status. When hunting, they experience failure
before they are consistently successful. Among whales, social creatures so much of their lives, young males must leave the pod of their
birth before they claim membership in a new pod with a mate. As
wild horses become yearlings, they band together, away from the
brood mares and stallion, returning only after reaching full maturity.
Grown, they join—or establish—new groups, but only after having
become at least temporarily distant from the safety of their original,

Photo by Michael Weisbrot

young-protecting families.

Don't we do much the same? I know that my teen must move away from me in order to remain close. He must learn his own capabilities by exercising them. Depending on me now reduces his opportunities to learn because of the known security my decisions represent. A safe haven, of course, but one with built-in limitations—for both of us.

As he grows, so do I. Thus, as I progress through my second teen experience, I am learning anew how important each of us is to the other and how important each of us is to ourselves.

There was a time when the empty nest was a period much feared by women whose primary identity was tied to their children's needs for nurturing. I am learning to anticipate an altered nest. It will contract and expand as the number of persons seeking comfort within it changes. But it can never be empty, as long as each of its original members retains his soul-touching. Such contact does not depend on physical presence or specific hours of shared space. Rather, our values and thoughts and dreams for one another will keep us close, even as we learn (and one of us relearns) how to swim alone.

The teen years are an intoxicating transition from near-total dependence to more distant interdependence—a recognition of the independent actions of our children as having adult value in themselves. In the midst of one person's seeking to set aside childhood, I am enjoying the rebirth of my own younger years.

Aren't we all time-travelers throughout our lives, moving to old age and returning to childhood by turns? Perhaps adolescence stands out only because it occurs with more obvious changes, more movement in all directions, than other phases. Therein lies its uniqueness. I feel privileged to be experiencing it once more.

24

EMPTY NEST

Penny Colman

My mother says that when I left home for college, she shut the door to my room and did not open it again until I returned for Thanksgiving. Even with the door shut, she still cried every time she walked by my room. I never knew that. Neither did anyone else—for, as she confessed years later, she never told a soul.

I found all this out on the day I took my oldest son to college. On my way home, I stopped at my mother's restaurant. "You need a bowl of chicken soup," she said when she saw my eyes brimming with tears. As I ate, she recalled her own pain. "I still hate it when you leave," she concluded. "Even after all these years."

My mother's nest emptied out much slower than mine. She had five children over the course of nineteen years; I had three children in two years—one plus twins. Either way, it makes little difference. An empty nest is an empty nest. Quiet. Very quiet.

True, an empty nest is neater. Even peaceful. There is something to be said for the freedom from juggling multiple schedules and needs. There is also the fun of cheering children on to new adventures and the satisfaction felt as they successfully establish their adult lives.

I celebrate all these positive feelings. But I also feel sad. And sometimes the sadness spreads across my chest and sinks into my bone marrow. Other women confess similar feelings, but only when I ask them directly. It is not modern to talk about such things. We contemporary mothers do not cling to our children. No empty nest syndrome for us; we are not going to fall apart when our children leave home. After all, we have books to write, legal briefs to file, degrees to earn, art to create, and trips to take.

Indeed we do. But we also have this profound event to deal with— this transition of our children from our daily lives to their own. From

Photo by Hildegard Adler

our nests to their nests. From childhood to adulthood. From being mothers up close to being mothers long distance. No more listening for late-night footsteps; no more allocating of chores; no more keeping track of who is eating what, when; and no more piles of dirty laundry. Our children's departure signals our retirement from the routine responsibilities of daily mothering.

Of course, it does not signal our retirement from caring, sharing, and loving. Our lives will still touch, hopefully often. Our children will return home to visit; they may even live with us for a while. But as adults.

Unfortunately, this time of transition goes unrecognized and unmarked in a mother's life. There is no gold watch, no letters of appreciation, and no pension. It is no wonder mothers such as my friend Pat—who raised four healthy, successful, and independent young adults—feel alone when their nests empty out and ask the question, "What have I done with my life?" It is no wonder my friend Suzi is scrambling to catch up financially after concentrating on raising her son and daughter. And it is no wonder my mother kept her pain a secret, although that was probably fortuitous. If she had told a physician or mental health professional, she most likely would have been labeled neurotic and handed a refillable prescription for Valium or some similar drug.

It took my own empty nest to jolt me into realizing the magnitude of the transition. Rationally, I was prepared: I had changed careers from one that did not fulfill my needs to one that did. Psychologically, I had no problem developing a lively, satisfying long-distance relationship with my sons or enjoying the new sense of freedom with my husband. But still there is the sadness. A tear here and there that surprises me—usually around dinnertime, when the loudest sound now is boiling water. A longing that catches me off guard. A hole in my soul that mostly stays shut but sometimes opens wide.

When that happens, I call Pat or Suzi. "Do you miss your kids so much it sometimes hurts?" I ask.

"Yes," comes the answer.

We catch our breath in the silence and then go on to talk about what else is happening in our lives.

25

MY TEEN YEARS

Juliana Korte

Today, at twenty-two, I feel focused and confident. And yet I think my teenage years were the hardest years of my life. Don't get me wrong. Compared with some, I had a relatively easy time of it. I got some bad grades, had my heart broken, and made some mistakes. I don't believe that anyone can go through his or her teenage years without experiencing a lot of change and making mistakes. The transformation starts around age fourteen or fifteen and is frighteningly sudden. Overnight, it seems, you start worrying about college, breaking away from your parents, boyfriends and girlfriends, being popular, and just plain fitting in somewhere.

My friends today don't believe me when I tell them what got me through those hard years. My parents. Yeah, those people you try to avoid in high school. I was fortunate that my parents weren't like most: they respected the changes I was going through. This is not to say that we saw eye to eye on everything, because we didn't.

Parents should understand that the teenage years are a time when they have to step back and let their teenagers make their own mistakes. I understand that it's hard for parents to see their kids in pain and that it's natural to want to shield them from any sadness. But parents can grow as their teenagers grow; they can learn to accept the fact that they can't and shouldn't shield their children from everything bad, the way they tried to when their kids were babies. The best thing a parent can do is listen, be there, and reserve judgment.

I can't tell you how many times nowadays I've looked back and regretted not following my parents' advice. But as a teenager, I had to learn for myself and make the decisions that I thought were best at the time.

Here's an example. During grade school and junior high, I went to a

Photo by Michael Weisbrot

private Catholic school. This was for educational rather than religious reasons. When it came time for me to choose a high school, I was given the choice of going to a public high school, provided that I progressed satisfactorily there, or to a Catholic high school that I would have had to commute to. My parents suggested that the all-girl Catholic high school would be a better choice than the local public high school, which was known to be lacking academically. But I chose the public high school, a fact that I regret thoroughly now. The high school administration didn't care what I did; it cared only about the kids in sports and advanced placement classes. I skipped a class once every few weeks, and the only action the school took was to telephone a recorded message to my house. Well, the phone number listed for our home was incorrect for all my high school years. By the time I reached my senior year, I didn't have enough credits to graduate and was forced to take night classes, in addition to my regular schoolwork, to make up the credits.

Today, I can't recall anything that I learned in high school. It just seems to have been three years of boyfriends and laziness. I have paid the price in college and have had to spend time learning things that I should have learned in high school. My first year in college would have been much easier with a good high school education. But happily, I don't think a bad high school education will keep me from getting my degree in accounting management and my CPA certificate. Mom and Dad, you were right. I should have gone to the Catholic high school and gotten a good education.

Although I think my parents were generally very helpful, as a teenager I had trouble at times communicating with them. When teenagers learn that they have some opinions that differ from those of their parents, they may think that no compromise is possible. But it is okay for parents and their teenagers to have opposite opinions. Situations like curfews and car use do require rules and regulations, because teenagers need to develop a sense of responsibility. I was grounded many times for coming home late. At the time, I didn't know why I insisted on being late. I just did. Finally it hit me...oh yeah...I need to show that I can act more responsibly before I will be allowed to do all the things I want to do. But no one could have told me that at the time. I had to find it out on my own, the hard way; otherwise it would have had no meaning for me.

The biggest lack of communication I experienced was between my teachers and myself. I was considered an average student by all of them, and for a long time I believed they were right. I'm not trying to blame teachers for all the bad grades I received, although they could have been more helpful and encouraging.

I felt lost as a teenager. Maybe this was because I didn't involved myself with school activities or because I wasn't part of the "in" crowd. I was then, and am still today, the type of person who wants to analyze everything: all the changes I was going through, what the future would hold for me, and why my life wasn't the way I wanted it to be.

Maybe my hopes were too high. I kept imagining the kind of life I thought would be ideal. I imagined my high school years would be like a Pepsi commercial, with a group of teenagers laughing and talking in a local hamburger stand. But I only had a few moments like that. I went to the prom my junior and senior years, as well as to various other dances. I had two boyfriends; each relationship lasted about two years. I got okay grades and had a few friends. But still I didn't feel like I was in the right place.

Maybe I felt this way because I always looked toward the future. Even when I was seventeen, I knew that my high school years hadn't been the best years of my life, the way everyone else was saying they were. I can recall sitting at a street light with one of my boyfriends in his Ford pickup. He revved the engine; this was Saturday night heaven in Longmont, Colorado. As the engine roared, I got this matter-of-fact thought in my head. "Now, why am I doing this?" I asked myself. Even then, I knew I didn't fit as a teenager.

I always knew that after high school, the world was mine and I could do whatever I wanted with it. Even when my senior-year boyfriend talked about "our life together...married" and how he would race cars and I would have his children, I always knew there was more to life than that. There had to be. One reason I don't think that I complained as much as I could have was that by holding onto my dream of being my own person, I felt perfectly content.

What I call "getting it together" didn't happen to me until I was twenty or twenty-one. I can remember almost the exact moment that it happened. After moving fifty miles from home to a big city, I was by myself in my own apartment. I had to deal with the fact that I was alone. What I did from then on was my own choice, and I had to use my own power to accomplish it. It takes a lot of thinking and soul

Photo by Suzanne Arms Wimberley

searching to find out who you are and what you want. I've been told
by people older than I am that some people never figure it out.

Maybe it was a desire for my own peace of mind that kept me from
trying drugs when I was a teenager. I may have just been one of the
lucky ones. Whatever the reason, I never wanted to use drugs. I saw
them being used at parties, and I knew that girls were using them in
the rest room at school. Yet I was never invited to try them. Neither
did I want to. I do know that drugs became an issue for some of my
friends. Everyone around me seemed to feel pressured to smoke
cigarettes, drink alcohol, or take drugs. It was never clear to me why
they put so much time and energy into something that they didn't
seem to want to do in the first place. Even one of my boyfriends told
me that magazine articles were wrong to say that marijuana was harmful. Whether or not that was the case, I still didn't want him smoking

it while he was seeing me. He never seemed to understand this.

The basic problem with teenagers and sex is that our bodies develop much faster than our minds. I've never been a parent, but the best advice I could give on this issue is: don't condone sex for your teenagers, but if they decide they want to be sexually active, make sure they know about birth control. As everyone surely knows by now, the teenage pregnancy rate in the United States is astoundingly high. I think one reason for this is a lack of knowledge about birth control, and another reason is that parents often say, "No, you can't do this," without acknowledging the fact that their teens may do it anyway.

I don't recall complaining very often as a teenager, although my parents may remember differently. I just accepted that I had to go to school and cope with the difficulties of being a teenager. I know I did complain about my older brothers. We seemed to have nothing in common. Everything that they did always seemed to be better than what I did, and since they were older they could do more things than I could. My brothers thought I got away with murder. Once we all left home and established our own lives, we became instant friends. It was as if we had never had any conflict. I feel that's the way it's supposed to be. My friends' biggest complaints were about their parents. They felt that they should be able to have more freedom and less pressure about grades. Everything revolved around their report cards. Some of them even did "bad" things (drugs, alcohol, etc.) to relieve the pressure.

My teenage years would have been better if I had the knowledge then that I have now. Of course, that's wishful thinking. Even though I was the youngest of four children and my parents already had practice dealing with teens, there were new experiences they had to deal with with me, because I was the only girl. I think if I had just realized that my parents weren't the bad guys in all of this, my teen years would have been better. After all, my mom and dad raised me the best way they knew how.

My advice to parents is first and foremost to let your teenagers make mistakes. Teens have to learn the hard way. They learn best that way. There are going to be tough times for you as parents because you won't always have the answers. That's okay. Drugs, sex, grades, friends— these are all issues teens have to deal with. Teenagers can't be told things that they need to learn on their own. Guide your kids and be their friend, not their policeman.

I had to deal with all these issues and more. I made mistakes and had hard times, but I learned from my experiences. I think I've turned out pretty normal, all things considered. My parents now tell me they always knew I would be fine. Looking back, I guess I wouldn't have done it any other way.

26

THE KIDS ARE ALL RIGHT

Diana Korte

Adolescence sometimes sounds like a disease for which there's no cure. Potheads, drunks, the kids who ditch classes or race up and down America's Main Streets—those are who we hear about. And it's all because of peer pressure. At least that's what we often say when we don't like the results.

But what about the teens who make the honor society, play the clarinet in the band, or finish their homework? Well, that's different, we say. Those are the kids who take after mom and dad. Turns out they are the majority.

Contrary to myth, most teens don't reject their parents' values. So says Daniel Offer of Chicago's Michael Reese Hospital, a nationally known psychiatrist who's researched "normal" teenagers for more than twenty years. Most teens, he claims, are not in turmoil or at the mercy of their impulses—even though they *are* influenced by their friends.

So why do we hear mostly about teens in trouble—teen suicides, alcoholics, and murderers? The media appears to love bad news, for one. But also, the approximately 20 percent of teens who are not well adjusted is a sizable number—about 3,500,000. These are certainly enough problem kids to keep media headlines harping about our troubled youth.

Of course, the 80 percent who are not especially troubled do have the usual anxieties we can all probably remember from our own adolescent days. Among those are taking exams, getting jobs, and going on dates. But then there's no age group in the life cycle that doesn't have problems to deal with.

Alcohol use and experimentation with drugs like marijuana certainly involve more than 20 percent of the teen population. What's

Photo by Michael Weisbrot

the likelihood that your children will indulge on a regular basis? "Most studies show," says Dr. Offer, "that kids who drink come from families that drink. If the parents don't drink, neither do the kids."

"Yes, kids do smoke a fair amount of marijuana," Offer continues, "but then parents have medicine cabinets full of all kinds of junk, prescribed maybe, but all kinds of tranquilizers. Valium is the most prescribed medication in the world." Whether we like it or not, we do serve as our children's models.

"Good family harmony is the best inoculation against major problems, whether emotional or having to do with delinquency or drugs," says Offer. "If parents are not there as a buffer zone, peer pressure can make a difference."

Peer pressure is definitely not all bad. We're probably never free of peer influence ourselves. It exists in our adult world—the proverbial "keeping up with the Joneses." Our adult fashions often reflect the same monotony as our teen's jeans and T-shirts. But much peer pressure is enhancing. Some teens are encouraged by their friends to do well in school and pursue healthy interests.

Still, often in the best circumstances, adolescence presents problematic issues for both teens and parents. These often revolve around the teen's search for freedom and the parent's need for some control. Parents might recognize the teen's need to grow up, but some still want to enforce the rules that were appropriate when Junior was nine years old but are no longer now that he's fourteen.

Just as the teen copes with new urges, his parents need to shift gears to a new role. "I spend the first twelve years of a child's life giving absolute directions. 'Yes, you can play at a friend's house' or 'It's time to come in and take a bath.' But after the age of twelve, I have to ease back," says Denver's Rhondda Hartman, author and mother of five young adults. "From then on, it becomes his world. I can't be so absolute anymore. I'm still directing when appropriate, but mostly I support and bolster my teenagers, offer them guidance. They certainly don't need a lot of criticism."

Whether teenagers are in the early junior high years or have advanced to post-high school, the optimistic among them fare best in their passage to adulthood.

"Friends and family are important to me, and I love fun and excitement," wrote one teenager for a school assignment. "Although many adults think that the teen years are a bad phase for us, they aren't.

True, for some kids it's hard, but for many it's a time for making friends and making new discoveries. Those adults who think we're going through a bad time must see only those who ruin it for us all, because people who look for the bad will surely find it. I say look for the best and we'll give it to you."

The kids are all right.

27

TEENS' GOLDEN RULES
FOR PARENTS

Diana Korte

Treat your teenagers as though they were your best friends. Make a conscious effort to demonstrate again and again how much you like your teens. After all, you don't shout and scream at a friend; why shout at your kids?

Trust your teenagers. When you say, and believe, that you trust your children in any situation, they carry your confidence with them. In order for this rule to be successful, they must understand clearly what behavior you consider appropriate. Don't set them up for failure by expecting them to read your mind. If you always suspect the worst of your children, they just may fulfill your prophecy.

Give your teenagers a good reputation to live up to. Keep expectations high and recriminations low. Offer lots of praise. Teens thrive on positive reinforcement—just as the rest of us do.

Let your teenagers solve their own problems. Be patient. Help when you're asked, but don't interfere in ordinary matters. It's normal for kids to get burned and make mistakes. You and I did, too. Be watchful, however, of major negative changes in their lives (plummeting grades or sudden loss of friends) in case they are your teens' cry for help.

Enjoy your teenagers. Keep their lives in perspective. Don't keep expecting trouble. It's too easy, especially for moms, to worry through their teen's normal new experiences from the first day of junior high, to driving the car, to going off to college.

Listen to your teenagers. Hear them out. Listen to how they say things and to what they say. Talking with them and helping them

Photo by Michael Weisbrot

with those feelings are as important as putting a kiss and a Band-Aid on the hurt knee of a six-year-old.

Know that your example counts. Like mother, like daughter. Like father, like son. Whether it's driving within the speed limit, being honest in your daily life, or using drugs and alcohol, remember that what you are and what you do speaks so loudly your children can't hear what you say.

Give your teenagers responsibility at home. Doing household chores helps younger teens know they can manage some things in the adult world, but don't expect them to agree with that or even want to help at home.

Never give up on your teenagers. Keep talking. They have to know that they are worth that much to you. All problems have solutions. Some are easy, but some are tough, and we don't always know what the answer is. That's when you can teach your kids how to cope—an essential skill for people of all ages.

Let your kids know that you have crises in your life, too. All of us face new issues and constant change. There's never a time when we have it all together—even as adults.

Spend time with your teenagers. It's easier, of course, to spend time with several family members at once. But there's much to gain from knowing your child on a one-to-one basis. According to a Cornell University study in the 1980s, the average suburban middle-class father spends only five minutes a week alone with each child—not counting watching television together or sharing mealtime. Mom, on the other hand, spends three hours a week alone with each child.

Appreciate your teenagers for who they really are. Know who your child is before he or she leaves your home to live in the world. It is common for your teens to be different from the people you thought they were, or perhaps from the people you wanted them to be. Be sure and let them know who you are, too.

28

CONTRIBUTORS

Adele Faber is the coauthor, with Elaine Mazlish, of the best-selling *How to Talk So Kids Will Listen and Listen So Kids Will Talk* and *Siblings Without Rivalry*. Her group workshop programs and video series, based on her books, are currently being used by thousands of groups worldwide. She travels throughout the United States and Canada presenting lectures and workshops on better ways of communicating with children and is the mother of three grown children.

Peggy O'Mara is the editor and publisher of *Mothering* magazine. She is also a poet and a writer. Her children are Lally, Finnie, Bram, and Nora.

Eda LeShan is an educator, family counselor, and award-winning author of numerous books for parents and children. She lives in New York City with her husband, Lawrence, a research and clinical psychologist. The LeShans are the parents of an adult daughter, Wendy, and the grandparents of Rhiannon.

Joyce Roby Belanger has been an elementary schoolteacher for eighteen years, as well as mother to her son, Zachary. She lives in Richmond, California, with her husband, Charles, a practitioner of traditional Chinese medicine.
"The Emerging Adolescent" first appeared in *Mothering* #42 (Winter 1987).

Betty K. Staley is the author of *Ow and the Crystal Clear* (currently out of print) and *A Bit of Heaven on the Earth* and coauthor of *Ariadne's Awakening* (Hawthorn Press, 1986). She has been a Waldorf teacher for more than twenty years and founded the Sacramento

Waldorf High School sixteen years ago. In addition to teaching in the high school, Betty lectures extensively and directs Waldorf High School Teacher Training at Rudolf Steiner College in Fair Oaks, California. Her three children, Andrea, George, and Sonya, are in their twenties.

"Character Development during Adolescence" was published in *Mothering* #49 (Fall 1988). It was excerpted with permission from *Between Form and Freedom: A Practical Guide to the Teenage Years* by Betty K. Staley (Stroud, U.K.: Hawthorn, 1988). This book is available from Hearthsong, P.O. Box B, Sebastopol, CA 95473.

David Elkind is Professor of Child Study at Tufts University in Medford, Massachusetts. His most recent books include *The Hurried Child*, *Miseducation*, and *Grandparenting*.

Lynda Madaras has taught teens and preteens about puberty and sex for more than ten years. She is the author of numerous books, including *The What's Happening to My Body? Books for Girls and Boys*, *Womancare*, and *Lynda Madaras Talks to Teens about AIDS*.

"The Changes of Puberty: Talking to Teens About What's Happening to Their Bodies" has been excerpted with permission from the introduction to *The "What's Happening to My Body?" Book for Boys* (New York: Newmarket Press, 1988) and *The "What's Happening to My Body?" Book for Girls* (New York: Newmarket Press, 1988).

Marion Cohen is a poet, writer, teacher, mathematician, and home schooling mother. Among other things, she writes about childhood, motherhood, pregnancy loss, and the feminist politics of the oppression of mothers as a class. Two of her latest books are *Counting to Zero* (Center for Thanatology Research, 1989) and *The Sitting-Down Hug* (The Liberal Press, 1989). She is the mother of four living children and the wife of a physicist with multiple sclerosis.

"Elle at Fourteen" first appeared in *Mothering* #56 (Summer 1990).

Ruth Lampert, M.A., M.F.C.C., is a psychotherapist in private practice and an adjunct professor at Pepperdine University Graduate School of Education and Psychology. She plans and presents sexuality education programs for public and private schools, conducts workshops, writes articles and audiotapes on a variety of subjects, and is

currently writing a book on single parenting. She is the founder and
director of Family Kaleidoscope, a therapy and training center in West
Los Angeles, California, where she lives. Ruth has four children and
five grandchildren.
"Sexuality Education with Adolescents" first appeared in *Mothering*
#48 (Summer 1988).

Candy Schock is a free-lance author and poet. She is the managing
editor for a parenting magazine and is working on her third novel.
Her work has appeared in *Bitterroot, Amelia, National Catholic
Reporter, Mutated Virus,* and the *J. D. MacDonald Bibliophile.*
"Puberty's Child" first appeared in *Mothering* #55 (Spring 1990).

Lorraine Vissering lives in Hyde Park, Vermont, with her husband,
David, and daughters, Carrie Chapline and Sia Ellyn. Carrie attends
the local Waldorf School. Lorraine works at a shelter for battered
women and their children, where she is the children's services coor-
dinator.

Don Dinkmeyer, Ph.D., is president of the Communication and
Motivation Training Institute and has written twenty-three books. He
lives with his wife, E. Jane, in Coral Springs, Florida. They have two
married sons, Don and Jim, and grandchildren, Luke, Drew, Joshua,
Caitlin, and Stephanie.
"Parents and Teens" first appeared in *Mothering* #34 (Winter 85).

Tovaa Steckull, M.S.C., M.S.W., an Interfaith minister of spiritual
counseling, has been privileged to nurture one child, now grown. She
spends much of her time in counseling, cross-cultural healing, multi-
media arts and crafts, and writing. Her writings have been published
in *The Women's Record, Up Against The Wall, In Memory of an
Unknown Child,* and *To Your Health Magazine.* She feels a special love
for children, older people, and the beauty and mystery of this planet.
"Adolescence" first appeared in *Mothering* #42 (Winter 87).

Elizabeth Hormann is a family counselor, lactation consultant, and
writer living in Cologne, Germany. A contributing editor to *Mothering,* she is the mother of five children and the grandmother of one.
"When Your Child Is Troubled" first appeared in *Mothering* #55
(Spring 1990).

"Communicating with Your Adolescent" first appeared in *Mothering #25* (Spring 1982).

Mitch Bobrow, M.S.W., lives with his wife and three children in Ithaca, New York, where he has a private psychotherapy practice. His first book, *Habit Breakthrough*, describes a holistic approach to breaking unwanted habits like overeating, procrastinating, and smoking. *Listening in Metaphor*, his second book, focuses on healing and understanding communication breakdowns.

Susannah Sheffer is the editor of *Growing Without Schooling* magazine and *A Life Worth Living: Selected Letters of John Holt* (Ohio State University Press, 1990). Her writings have appeared in *The Progressive*, *Mothering*, *The American School Board Journal*, and other publications.

Robert Schwebel, Ph.D., is a psychologist in Tucson, Arizona. He lectures and conducts workshops on the topic of alcohol and other drugs. He is the author of *Saying No Is Not Enough: Raising Children Who Make Wise Decisions about Drugs and Alcohol* (New York: Newmarket Press, 1989). He is the coauthor of *A Guide to a Happier Family* (Los Angeles: J. P. Tarcher, Inc., 1989).

Ross Herbertson leads weekly rock climbing trips for teens. He lives at Slide Ranch, an environmental and agricultural teaching farm in Muir Beach, California, with his wife, Sue, and their two sons, Benjamin and Jeffrey. The quotes appearing at the end of this article were recorded verbatim.

"Rock Climbing" first appeared in *Mothering #55* (Spring 1990).

Bruce Bassoff is Professor of English at the University of Colorado. He is a published playwright, author of scholarly books and articles, and author of books for young people, including *Supercharged*, published in 1990 by Bookmakers Guild. He has also contributed to *Being a Father* (Santa Fe, N.M.: John Muir Publications, 1990), an anthology of essays about fathering. He lives in Boulder, Colorado, with his wife, Evelyn, and their children, Leah and Jonathan.

Evelyn Silten Bassoff is a psychologist in private practice and Adjunct Professor of Education at the University of Colorado. She has contributed to *Mothering* and is the author of *Mothers and Daughters: Loving and Letting Go* (A Plume Book, New American Library, 1988) and *Mothering Ourselves: Help and Healing for Adult Daughters* (Dutton, 1991). She lives in Boulder, Colorado, with her husband, Bruce, and their children, Leah and Jonathan.

Geeta Dardick, a member of the American Society of Journalists and Authors, specializes in writing articles on family issues. Her work has appeared in *Reader's Digest, Family Circle, Woman's Day, East West Journal, Sierra*, and many other national magazines. Her article, "Home Study and the Public Schools," was included in *Mothering*'s recent book *Schooling at Home: Parents, Kids, and Learning* (Santa Fe, N.M.: John Muir Publications, 1990). A back-to-the-land farmer, Ms. Dardick's book, *Home Butchering and Meat Preservation* (TAB Books, 1986), details a methodology for raising farm animals consciously.
   "The Twenty-Five-Year Commitment" first appeared in *Mothering* #42 (Winter 1987).

Joan Logghe, poet and teacher of writing, is poetry editor for *Mothering* magazine. She has held writing workshops in New Mexico and nationally, and her students have included the elderly, prisoners, and the Women's Wellness Retreat. Joan and her husband, Michael, are committed to gardening, conservation, and their family, Corina, Matt, and Hope.

Daryl Allen is employed by an architectural firm in Santa Cruz, California, which studies and restores all types of historic buildings in the Southwest. She has published several articles about historical architecture. Her son, now in his twenties, is a musician and works in a recording studio.
   "To My Son" first appeared in *Mothering* #13 (Fall 1979).

Kathleen Auerbach, Ph.D., I.B.C.L.C., is a lactation consultant, editor-in-chief of the *Journal of Human Lactation*, and a free-lance lecturer, editor, and author. She is a contributing editor of *Mothering* and the mother of a son.
   "Trust, Responsibility, and Letting Go" is an edited compilation of "Trust and Responsibility," which first appeared in *Mothering* #49 (Fall

1988) and "Teens: The Second Time Around," which was published in *Mothering* #37 (Fall 1985).

Penny Colman is a writer, speaker, and educator living in Englewood, New Jersey, with her husband, Bob. Their departed nestlings are Jonathan, David, and Stephen. Her books for children include *I Never Do Anything Bad* and *Dark Closets and Noises in the Night* (both from Paulist Press) and *Dorothea Dix: A Life of Purpose* (Betterway Publications).

"Empty Nest" first appeared in *Mothering* #55 (Spring 1990).

Juliana Korte is a student at the University of Colorado at Denver and the daughter of Diana Korte, another contributor to this book.

Diana Korte produces public radio documentaries and writes for magazines and newspapers. She is the coauthor of *A Good Birth, A Safe Birth* and the author of *Choices in Women's Health: An A-Z Guide* (1991). She and her husband, Gene Korte, live in Boulder, Colorado. They have four children, Neil, Drew, Aren, and Juliana, who is also a contributor to this book.

"The Kids Are All Right" and "Teens' Golden Rules for Parents" first appeared in *Mothering* #37 (Fall 1985).

Other Books from John Muir Publications

Adventure Vacations: From Trekking in New Guinea to Swimming in Siberia, Richard Bangs (65-76-9) 256 pp. $17.95

Asia Through the Back Door, 3rd ed., Rick Steves and John Gottberg (65-48-3) 326 pp. $15.95

Being a Father: Family, Work, and Self, Mothering Magazine (65-69-6) 176 pp. $12.95

Buddhist America: Centers, Retreats, Practices, Don Moreale (28-94-X) 400 pp. $12.95

Bus Touring: Charter Vacations, U.S.A., Stuart Warren with Douglas Bloch (28-95-8) 168 pp. $9.95

California Public Gardens: A Visitor's Guide, Eric Sigg (65-56-4) 304 pp. $16.95 (Available 3/91)

Catholic America: Self-Renewal Centers and Retreats, Patricia Christian-Meyer (65-20-3) 325 pp. $13.95

Complete Guide to Bed & Breakfasts, Inns & Guesthouses, Pamela Lanier (65-43-2) 520 pp. $16.95

Costa Rica: A Natural Destination, Ree Strange Sheck (65-51-3) 280 pp. $15.95

Elderhostels: The Students' Choice, Mildred Hyman (65-28-9) 224 pp. $12.95 (2nd ed. available 5/91 $15.95)

Environmental Vacations: Volunteer Projects to Save the Planet, Stephanie Ocko (65-78-5) 240 pp. $14.95

Europe 101: History & Art for the Traveler, 4th ed., Rick Steves and Gene Openshaw (65-79-3) 372 pp. $15.95

Europe Through the Back Door, 9th ed., Rick Steves (65-42-4) 432 pp. $16.95

Floating Vacations: River, Lake, and Ocean Adventures, Michael White (65-32-7) 256 pp. $17.95

Gypsying After 40: A Guide to Adventure and Self-Discovery, Bob Harris (28-71-0) 264 pp. $14.95

The Heart of Jerusalem, Arlynn Nellhaus (28-79-6) 336 pp. $12.95

Indian America: A Traveler's Companion, Eagle/Walking Turtle (65-29-7) 424 pp. $16.95 (2nd ed. available 7/91 $16.95)

Mona Winks: Self-Guided Tours of Europe's Top Museums, Rick Steves and Gene Openshaw (28-85-0) 456 pp. $14.95

Opera! The Guide to Western Europe's Great Houses, Karyl Lynn Zietz (65-81-5) 280 pp. $18.95 (Available 4/91)

Paintbrushes and Pistols: How the Taos Artists Sold the West, Sherry C. Taggett and Ted Schwarz (65-65-3) 280 pp. $17.95

The People's Guide to Mexico, 8th ed., Carl Franz (65-60-2) 608 pp. $17.95

The People's Guide to RV Camping in Mexico, Carl Franz with Steve Rogers (28-91-5) 320 pp. $13.95

Preconception: A Woman's Guide to Preparing for Pregnancy and Parenthood, Brenda E. Aikey-Keller (65-44-0) 232 pp. $14.95

Ranch Vacations: The Complete Guide to Guest and Resort, Fly-Fishing, and Cross-Country Skiing Ranches, Eugene Kilgore (65-30-0) 392 pp. $18.95 (2nd ed. available 5/91 $18.95)

Schooling at Home: Parents, Kids, and Learning, *Mothering* Magazine (65-52-1) 264 pp. $14.95

The Shopper's Guide to Art and Crafts in the Hawaiian Islands, Arnold Schuchter (65-61-0) 272 pp. $13.95

The Shopper's Guide to Mexico, Steve Rogers and Tina Rosa (28-90-7) 224 pp. $9.95

Ski Tech's Guide to Equipment, Skiwear, and Accessories, edited by Bill Tanler (65-45-9) 144 pp. $11.95

Ski Tech's Guide to Maintenance and Repair, edited by Bill Tanler (65-46-7) 160 pp. $11.95

Teens: A Fresh Look, *Mothering* Magazine (65-54-8) 240 pp. $14.95

A Traveler's Guide to Asian Culture, Kevin Chambers (65-14-9) 224 pp. $13.95

Traveler's Guide to Healing Centers and Retreats in North America, Martine Rudee and Jonathan Blease (65-15-7) 240 pp. $11.95

Understanding Europeans, Stuart Miller (65-77-7) 272 pp. $14.95

Undiscovered Islands of the Caribbean, 2nd ed., Burl Willes (65-55-6) 232 pp. $14.95

Undiscovered Islands of the Mediterranean, Linda Lancione Moyer and Burl Willes (65-53-X) 232 pp. $14.95

A Viewer's Guide to Art: A Glossary of Gods, People, and Creatures, Marvin S. Shaw and Richard Warren (65-66-1) 152 pp. $10.95

2 to 22 Days Series
These pocket-size itineraries (4½″ × 8″) are a refreshing departure from ordinary guidebooks. Each offers 22 flexible daily itineraries that can be used to get the most out of vacations of any length. Included are not only "must see" attractions but also little-known villages and hidden "jewels" as well as valuable general information.

22 Days Around the World, Roger Rapoport and Burl Willes (65-31-9) 200 pp. $9.95 (1992 ed. available 8/91 $11.95)

2 to 22 Days Around the Great Lakes, 1991 ed., Arnold Schuchter (65-62-9) 184 pp. $9.95

22 Days in Alaska, Pamela Lanier (28-68-0) 128 pp. $7.95

22 Days in the American Southwest, 2nd ed., Richard Harris (28-88-5) 176 pp. $9.95

22 Days in Asia, Roger Rapoport and Burl Willes (65-17-3) 136 pp. $7.95 (1992 ed. available 8/91 $9.95)

22 Days in Australia, 3rd ed., John Gottberg (65-40-8) 148 pp. $7.95 (1992 ed. available 8/91 $9.95)

22 Days in California, 2nd ed., Roger Rapoport (65-64-5) 176 pp. $9.95

22 Days in China, Gaylon Duke and Zenia Victor (28-72-9) 144 pp. $7.95

22 Days in Europe, 5th ed., Rick Steves (65-63-7) 192 pp. $9.95

22 Days in Florida, Richard Harris (65-27-0) 136 pp. $7.95 (1992 ed. available 8/91 $9.95)

22 Days in France, Rick Steves (65-07-6) 154 pp. $7.95 (1991 ed. available 4/91 $9.95)

22 Days in Germany, Austria & Switzerland, 3rd ed., Rick Steves (65-39-4) 136 pp. $7.95

22 Days in Great Britain, 3rd ed., Rick Steves (65-38-6) 144 pp. $7.95 (1991 ed. available 4/91 $9.95)

22 Days in Hawaii, 2nd ed., Arnold Schuchter (65-50-5) 144 pp. $7.95 (1992 ed. available 8/91 $9.95)

22 Days in India, Anurag Mathur (28-87-7) 136 pp. $7.95

22 Days in Japan, David Old (28-73-7) 136 pp. $7.95
22 Days in Mexico, 2nd ed., Steve Rogers and Tina Rosa (65-41-6) 128 pp. $7.95
22 Days in New England, Anne Wright (28-96-6) 128 pp. $7.95 (1991 ed. available 4/91 $9.95)
2 to 22 Days in New Zealand, 1991 ed., Arnold Schuchter (65-58-0) 192 pp. $9.95
22 Days in Norway, Sweden, & Denmark, Rick Steves (28-83-4) 136 pp. $7.95 (1991 ed. available 4/91 $9.95)
22 Days in the Pacific Northwest, Richard Harris (28-97-4) 136 pp. $7.95 (1991 ed. available 4/91 $9.95)
22 Days in the Rockies, Roger Rapoport (65-68-8) 176 pp. $9.95
22 Days in Spain & Portugal, 3rd ed., Rick Steves (65-06-8) 136 pp. $7.95
22 Days in Texas, Richard Harris (65-47-5) 176 pp. $9.95
22 Days in Thailand, Derk Richardson (65-57-2) 176 pp. $9.95
22 Days in the West Indies, Cyndy & Sam Morreale (28-74-5)136 pp. $7.95

"Kidding Around" Travel Guides for Young Readers
Written for kids eight years of age and older. Generously illustrated in two colors with imaginative characters and images. An adventure to read and a treasure to keep.

Kidding Around Atlanta, Anne Pedersen (65-35-1) 64 pp. $9.95
Kidding Around Boston, Helen Byers (65-36-X) 64 pp. $9.95
Kidding Around Chicago, Lauren Davis (65-70-X) 64 pp. $9.95
Kidding Around the Hawaiian Islands, Sarah Lovett (65-37-8) 64 pp. $9.95

Kidding Around London, Sarah Lovett (65-24-6) 64 pp. $9.95
Kidding Around Los Angeles, Judy Cash (65-34-3) 64 pp. $9.95
Kidding Around the National Parks of the Southwest, Sarah Lovett 108 pp. $12.95
Kidding Around New York City, Sarah Lovett (65-33-5) 64 pp. $9.95
Kidding Around Paris, Rebecca Clay (65-82-3) 64 pp. $9.95 (Available 4/91)
Kidding Around Philadelphia, Rebecca Clay (65-71-8) 64 pp. $9.95
Kidding Around San Francisco, Rosemary Zibart (65-23-8) 64 pp. $9.95
Kidding Around Santa Fe, Susan York (65-99-8) 64 pp. $9.95 (Available 5/91)
Kidding Around Seattle, Rick Steves (65-84-X) 64 pp. $9.95 (Available 4/91)
Kidding Around Washington, D.C., Anne Pedersen (65-25-4) 64 pp. $9.95

Environmental Books for Young Readers
Written for kids eight years of age and older. Examines the environmental issues and opportunities that today's kids will face during their lives.

The Indian Way: Learning to Communicate with Mother Earth, Gary McLain (65-73-4) 114 pp. $9.95
The Kids' Environment Book: What's Awry and Why, Anne Pedersen (55-74-2) 192 pp. $13.95
No Vacancy: The Kids' Guide to Population and the Environment, Glenna Boyd (61-000-7) 64 pp. $9.95 (Available 8/91)
Rads, Ergs, and Cheeseburgers: The Kids' Guide to Energy and the Environment, Bill Yanda (65-75-0) 108 pp. $12.95

"Extremely Weird" Series for Young Readers

Written for kids eight years of age and older. Designed to help kids appreciate the world around them. Each book includes full-color photographs with detailed and entertaining descriptions of the "extremely weird" creatures.

Extremely Weird Bats, Sarah Lovett (61-008-2) 48 pp. $9.95 (Available 7/91)
Extremely Weird Frogs, Sarah Lovett (61-006-6) 48 pp. $9.95 (Available 6/91)
Extremely Weird Spiders, Sarah Lovett (61-007-4) 48 pp. $9.95 (Available 6/91)

Automotive Repair Manuals

How to Keep Your VW Alive (65-80-7) 440 pp. $19.95
How to Keep Your Subaru Alive (65-11-4) 480 pp. $19.95
How to Keep Your Toyota Pickup Alive (28-81-3) 392 pp. $19.95
How to Keep Your Datsun/ Nissan Alive (28-65-6) 544 pp. $19.95

Other Automotive Books

The Greaseless Guide to Car Care Confidence: Take the Terror Out of Talking to Your Mechanic, Mary Jackson (65-19-X) 224 pp. $14.95
Off-Road Emergency Repair & Survival, James Ristow (65-26-2) 160 pp. $9.95

Ordering Information

If you cannot find our books in your local bookstore, you can order directly from us. Please check the "Available" date above. If you send us money for a book not yet available, we will hold your money until we can ship you the book. Your books will be sent to you via UPS (for U.S. destinations). UPS will not deliver to a P.O. Box; please give us a street address. Include $2.75 for the first item ordered and $.50 for each additional item to cover shipping and handling costs. For airmail within the U.S., enclose $4.00. All foreign orders will be shipped surface rate; please enclose $3.00 for the first item and $1.00 for each additional item. Please inquire about foreign airmail rates.

Method of Payment

Your order may be paid by check, money order, or credit card. We cannot be responsible for cash sent through the mail. All payments must be made in U.S. dollars drawn on a U.S. bank. Canadian postal money orders in U.S. dollars are acceptable. For VISA, MasterCard, or American Express orders, include your card number, expiration date, and your signature, or call (800) 888-7504. Books ordered on American Express cards can be shipped only to the billing address of the cardholder. Sorry, no C.O.D.'s. Residents of sunny New Mexico, add 5.875% tax to the total.

Address all orders and inquiries to:

John Muir Publications
P.O. Box 613
Santa Fe, NM 87504
(505) 982-4078
(800) 888-7504